T0065443

IS THIS THE BEST GOD COULD DO?

SARAH TIRRI

BALBOA.PRESS
A DIVISION OF HAY HOUSE

Copyright © 2021 Sarah Tirri.

All rights reserved. No part of this book may be used or reproduced by any means, graphic, electronic, or mechanical, including photocopying, recording, taping or by any information storage retrieval system without the written permission of the author except in the case of brief quotations embodied in critical articles and reviews.

Balboa Press books may be ordered through booksellers or by contacting:

Balboa Press
A Division of Hay House
1663 Liberty Drive
Bloomington, IN 47403
www.balboapress.com
844-682-1282

Because of the dynamic nature of the Internet, any web addresses or links contained in this book may have changed since publication and may no longer be valid. The views expressed in this work are solely those of the author and do not necessarily reflect the views of the publisher, and the publisher hereby disclaims any responsibility for them.

The author of this book does not dispense medical advice or prescribe the use of any technique as a form of treatment for physical, emotional, or medical problems without the advice of a physician, either directly or indirectly. The intent of the author is only to offer information of a general nature to help you in your quest for emotional and spiritual well-being. In the event you use any of the information in this book for yourself, which is your constitutional right, the author and the publisher assume no responsibility for your actions.

Any people depicted in stock imagery provided by Getty Images are models, and such images are being used for illustrative purposes only. Certain stock imagery © Getty Images.

Cover design: Sarah Tirr
Artist: Daniel Jankowski

Print information available on the last page.

ISBN: 978-1-9822-6079-8 (sc)
ISBN: 978-1-9822-6080-4 (e)

Balboa Press rev. date: 02/19/2021

Pleas visit my blog: www.sarahtirri.com
Contact the author: sarahtirri@gmail.com

CONTENTS

CHAPTER ONE

In the Beginning

I was in a bad mood, pre-menstrual and bitchy. I had turned my cold back on my husband the night before. I had yelled at my kids. I felt disgruntled, and negative thoughts plagued me. I couldn't be bothered to change the dogs' water bowl, and I couldn't be bothered to shower. I remained on the couch and looked to escape. I turned on the TV and watched the desperate or maladjusted reveal themselves to Jerry Springer. I watched the news: an assortment of third-world scarcity, including a load of sub-Saharan children who really didn't care whether they lived or died, first-world surplus, deadly epidemics, warfare, terrorist attacks, suicide bombings, opiate addiction, youth rebellion, earthquakes, overcrowded schools, homelessness, identity theft, global warming, stock market uncertainly, out of control brush fires, unemployment, illegal immigration, and political corruption. It was all depressing. I then changed the channel and watched a surgeon prepare to separate Siamese-twins while their mother agonized over the fact that she'd had to choose. I changed it again and saw live coverage of a prison riot, and then I watched a documentary about the binge-drinking culture that is cursing my motherland. *"Entertainment Television"* was my last stop; here I learned about Hollywood's most acrimonious divorces...............*"What a crap planet this is," I said to God out loud. "Is this the best you could do?"

CHAPTER TWO

Linda's Leaving

It began as a normal May morning until I telephoned my mother's doctor in the United Kingdom. I wanted to find out the results of the tests she had recently undergone. My mother had previously been diagnosed with a minor stroke.

"Hello. My name is Sarah Tirri, and I'm calling from Florida to find out the results of a recent MRI scan that my mother had."

"Hold the line. I'll put you through to radiology."

"Radiology, can I help you."

"Yes, I'm calling to find out the results of an MRI scan my mother had recently."

"Are you related to the patient?"

"Yes I am. I am her daughter."

"We are not allowed to give the results out over the phone. You will have to make an appointment to see the doctor."

"Well, that's a little tricky. I'd like to talk to the doctor over the phone. You see, I live in America and am not able to just pop in."

"Oh. I get it. Well, hang on a minute. I'll find out whether somebody can help you."

"Hello, this is Dr. Sherman's nurse. How can I help?"

"Yes. I'm calling to find out the results of an MRI scan my mother had recently."

"Your name please?"

"Sarah Tirri."

"Mrs. Tirri, it's not hospital policy to discuss a patient's medical diagnosis over the telephone."

"I understand that. But I live in Florida, and although I can fly to England if I need to, I have three young children, and my youngest is doing her first ballet recital, and my dog is in heat. My husband can watch my children, but he has this tricky deposition to get through two-hundred miles away in Miami. And if my mother's doing all right, I should like to plan my trip in a week or so."

"I see. Let me try and locate the doctor who's treating your mother."

"Thank you."

After several minutes, another female voice came on the line. "Hello, this is Dr. Clifford-Jones' nurse."

"Hello. My name is Sarah Tirri. I am calling from America and need to know the results of an MRI scan my mother had yesterday."

"Well, Dr. Clifford-Jones is in surgery at the moment. I'll see if there is another doctor who can help you."

"Thank you." I lit a cigarette.

"Operator. Where can I direct your call?"

"Shit! No! Operator? No! I'm sorry operator. I think I got disconnected. I was on hold."

"Who were you holding for?"

"I don't know; somebody who can help me."

"Who was the last person you were speaking to?"

"Dr. Clifford Jones' nurse."

"Hang on, madam. I'll try and re-connect you."

"Thanks."

"Hello, this is Doctor Clifford-Jones' nurse."

"Yes, this is Sarah Tirri again. I just spoke with you and…"

"Oh. Mrs. Tirri. Good. I thought I'd lost you. Hold the line.

I am going to connect you to Dr. Jacob." The line went dead again for a few moments.

"Hello Mrs. Tirri, Dr. Marcus Jacob here. Um, the nurse told me that you were looking to know the results of the MRI scan that your mother had Monday. Usually we don't discuss the results over the phone, but I understand you live in America. It's not hospital policy, and I want you to know that, but under the circumstances, I think I can make an exception."

"Is my mum okay?" I asked. There was a weighty pause.

"What is it that you know of your mother's condition, Mrs. Tirri?"

"Well, she had what was diagnosed as a transient ischemic attack a little over two months ago. I understand this to be a minor stoke, and Dr. Clifford-Jones suggested another scan as a precaution but didn't seem unduly worried."

There was another pause, but briefer this time. "Well, I am not sure how else to put this, but your mother didn't have a stroke. She has a massive brain tumor, and it is untreatable."

"A brain tumor?"

"Your mother's brain tumor is untreatable, Mrs. Tirri. She had an MRI two months ago, and a brain tumor was not detected at that time. Her cancer grew so quickly. I have never seen anything like it. I am so sorry."

I was shaking now, but my voice remained steady. "What about chemotherapy?"

"I'm sorry, but that won't make her better. There is nothing we can do to help her."

"How long has she got? How long has my mother got to live?

"The tumor will kill her within weeks."

"Weeks? How many weeks?"

"At the rate it's growing, a month—two—tops. I hate to tell

you this dreadful news over the telephone. This must be awful for you."

"Yes. It is. It's not your fault… I'm not quite sure what else to say. It's awful, isn't it? I'm going to go now. I have to go. Thank you." I hung up the phone and lit another cigarette.

It wasn't a minor stroke; it was a death sentence. I was stunned. I ground out my cigarette and lit another. My beloved mother was dying. She was going to bloody well die.

It took a few surreal hours before the news started sinking in, and then an appalling thought began to take form: My mother had no idea she was so ill, and I would have to tell her that, this time next month, she'd be dead… And so my husband and I made the inevitable, "this cannot be happening" trip to England. The process of trying to come to terms with the enormity of what was happening was alien and terrifying. We landed, groggy and apprehensive, and drove towards the hospital over the Sussex Downs. I tried to compose myself before seeing my mother and practiced many a serene, comforting smile. The hospital had recently been under major renovation, and its big new wing could be seen a mile away, but the neurological unit had been relegated to original building, which was tucked behind the Accident and Emergency Department. It was a typical Victorian affair: low ceilings, exposed plumbing, and peeling paintwork. The cooking smells and the vague noise of invisible dripping water added to the ambience, and so did Prince Charming's doubtful countenance. My husband was used to American hospitals with air conditioning, automatic doors, and faux greenery—a plush Hilton-kind of sterility. I found myself reassuring him that this was the "top neurological unit in the country," but I could tell from his expression that he wouldn't have a tooth removed in this joint.

My brother was waiting for us in the "lobby," and the nurse

directed us to our mother, who was sharing a ward with three other women. I cheerily greeted her and told her that her hair looked shiny and her cornflower blue nightgown suited her complexion. *Well, Sarah seems unruffled,* I could feel her ascertain. *Things can't be that bad.* Or maybe she knew the truth but stopped herself from saying, "Why the false joviality, Sarah? For fuck's sake I'm dying here. Be yourself. We haven't got much time left."

My brother and my husband stood uneasily, hoping for a diversion: a nurse, a phone call, an earthquake, the tea trolley, a power outage, anything. I sat on the edge of my mother's bed and watched as she desperately tried to glean information from the various hospital staff whose job it was to pretend to know nothing at all. I reassured her that the doctors were going to meet with us at noon. She immediately looked at the clock. It was 11:55. I told her we would come right back and let her know the prognosis. I left the ward, my brother and husband expounding relief in tow.

Although the eminent neurosurgeon with a double-barreled surname had actually misdiagnosed my mother's condition, my brother and I, for some strange reason, decided to leave her health in his questionable, but hopefully capable hands. Maybe he hadn't seen what any other neurosurgeon would also have not seen. Maybe diagnosing her with a stroke was the correct course of action. Maybe neurosurgeons with impressive surnames deserved their eminence, but they didn't deserve the rank of magician.

The doctor pointed across the room at about a dozen x-ray-type pictures tucked behind illuminated glass. My mother's brain was displayed in various poses. We stared ominously.

Betraying acute discomfort by his tone and his fidgeting, the doctor talked about the cancerous mass that he hadn't detected two months previously. He then prepared himself for a tirade of questions: Is there *any* hope? Is there a *chance* that you got it wrong again? Are you sure? Is it definitely malignant? Why won't chemo work? What is radiation? What have you told my mother? What would you do if she was *your* mother?

In a last-ditch attempt to avoid the inevitable, the neurosurgeon gave us a brief reprieve. There apparently remained a zillion-to-one chance that the tumor wasn't malignant. It was decided that one last biopsy would be prudent, and the procedure was scheduled for the following Wednesday. We were told that the odds of winning the lottery were better. But this act of denial was something for which we were grateful. My mother was dying, and the biopsy was irrelevant. But because this microchance represented the best prospect of a miracle, we all went along with the charade.

During this moment of reprieve, my mother willed things to get better. The nurses knew the truth, and so did the people who loved her. My mother found our evasiveness annoying, but she didn't want to face the truth either. The next three days drifted by: Sunday, Monday, Tuesday. My mother saw family members she hadn't seen for a while, and she tried to stay cheerful and optimistic. I played my part well, adding credence to the theater in the same way that any talented actress might.

Wednesday finally arrived, and although I didn't know it then, this would be the last time I would see my mother as I knew her. Anesthesia came first. Then her scalp was shaved. Next her head was clamped in a steel vice and her skull was penetrated by a drill-bit strong enough to bore through bone, after which the doctors scraped away a piece of the barnacle that had attached itself to the side of her brain. The specimen of cancer would then be sent away for analysis, and this would give us a couple more days.

The futile brain biopsy that we had all so readily agreed to accelerated my mother's decline, which I suppose happens when part of your brain gets hacked away. My brother and I had not considered the implications of invasive neurosurgery, and neither of us had considered how compromised our mother's immune system had become. I don't know how brutal the procedure actually was, but I *do* know that our mother was never the same again. In retrospect, there are two things I regret in my life, agreeing to the biopsy and not sending my mother more flowers.

The biopsy took three days to analyze, after which we were asked to meet with the doctor. His expression was solemn, and nobody said that much because nothing had changed. The doctor shuffled some paperwork and sighed in empathy. His job was over, and he shook our hands. It was now time to face our mother, and my brother and I walked towards her ward. I shall never forget that walk.

Mark and I sat on either side of my mother's bed. She was leaning forward expectantly. The doctor had already told my mother that the biopsy's results were not favorable, but because she had just been drilled through her head, she found processing information rather difficult. Her big, brown, beautiful eyes met mine. Tears stung as I heard myself say, "Things are not good, Mum." My brother and I couldn't bring ourselves to say the D-word. But we didn't need to.

"So it's curtains, then, is it?" my mother whispered. The pain on her children's faces confirmed her worst fears. My mother let out the breath she had been holding in for the last six days and started whimpering like a baby.

She was soon shipped off to the hospice to die, and, writhing in the grimness of it all, I flew back and forth between the U.S. and England. The woman who had given birth to me was leaving me behind. She was leaving me. She was going to bloody well leave me! "You selfish bitch Sarah," I said to myself. "It's not all about you. What about her? Look at her!"

I hated walking into the hospice. I hated seeing my mother sitting in the bay window with a tartan blanket over her knee. I hated watching her flip through magazines that were upside-down. I hated watching her manufacture serenity in an attempt to ward off dread. I hated watching her scoff food into her mouth. (She had been pumped with steroids and her appetite was through the roof.) She even ate the core of her tomato. She had never done that before. She had always been a delicate, finicky eater, choosy and selective. Now she was a savage, attacking whatever was set before her. The steroids had made her face puff up too. Her jaw line had extended, making her look mannish. I dreaded seeing her, and I dreaded the thought of not seeing her.

The tumor was as ravenous. In its desire to devour her from the inside out, it coursed through my mother so rapidly that the doctors told us it was the worst tumor they had ever seen. The massive lump of cancer began paralyzing my mother, first immobilizing her muscles, taking away the use of her right hand and then her right arm. It systematically worked its way through her body, crushing her brain in the process.

I boarded a plane for America and flew back to my children, and within eight hours, bought another ticket to fly back to England. I had two days to get through. I filled them with prayer and red wine. I spoke with my mother often—strange calls that mixed residual denial with stoic, stiff upper-lip bravery. My mother's condition was scary and so were my thoughts. My dread took me to levels of communication with God that I hadn't experienced before. I wasn't sure about God's role in any of this, and so I simply asked Him to cure my mother..."*Make her better, God. Stop this happening. Please!"* I called prayer lines and asked strangers to pray for my mother's healing. I read Bible passages that I thought might propel me into an epiphany of understanding. I touched the television screen when the evangelist told me I would feel the healing power of God. I prayed for a miracle.

Actually, I was told by my Christian friends that I must expect a miracle, and so, in a reverie I created one. Over and over it played out in my mind. My mother was going to smile serenely, I just knew it. She was going to slowly pull back the bedcovers and stretch like a cat. She would then slip out of bed and offer her delicate hand to a dashing young doctor who would graciously waltz her across the floor. But George Clooney didn't show up, just an overworked nurse who had seen it all before.

"What's happened to the miracle, God?" I would ask. "Don't let my mother die; she's only fifty-nine. Please, you're running out of time."

While I was preparing for my next trip to the United Kingdom, a close friend said with uncharacteristic urgency that she needed to tell me something. She gripped my shoulders and stared squarely into my eyes. She then asked me whether my mother had, at any time during her life, "received Jesus Christ as her Lord and Savior."

I didn't know the answer to this question. My mother had never really spoken of religious matters, but I assumed she either hadn't considered the matter at all or hadn't gotten around to it yet. My mother, who shared everything with me, hadn't particularly mentioned God or Jesus, and so it seemed unlikely.

In response to my indifferent shrug, the mood changed. My Christian friend held me still and looked into my eyes. Her delivery fervent, she told me that my mother must ask God to receive her into the kingdom of heaven and accept Jesus Christ as her Lord and Savior. I was to assist my mother—help her, reach her, shake her—her future lay in the balance. I was to convey to her the supreme necessity of making contact with God, because if she hadn't already, her failure to accomplish this "before death mission" would render her "not born again." According to my friend, not fulfilling this one-time edict ensured a torturous future of terrifying eternal pain.

"What are you saying? What if my mother doesn't get saved?" I asked my friend uneasily. Her furtive glance said it all.

Another Christian friend had defined exactly what *my* role in all this must be. Apparently, I must help my mother *receive* God, and until I achieved that feat, nothing else mattered. I packed my suitcase and pondered how I could get my mother to converse with her maker if she hadn't already done so. The Christians with whom I had consulted assured me that salvation rests on our ability to accomplish one simple task—accepting Jesus Christ as Lord and Savior. Forgiveness will follow, the buzzer will sound, and the pearly gates will swing wide open. St. Peter will wave you through as he fills out his inventory. Getting a tick in the "saved" column means all will be well and good. Getting a tick in the "unsaved" column means....

"Quick, cover your ears! That's Linda. Ignore her screams. She got her fingers caught when the gates slammed in her face. Silly woman. She didn't do very well. She's not saved. Jeffrey the serial killer knew the deal; he arrived here from death row yesterday morning. Even he had the wherewithal to get his arse saved before they fried him."

"No Linda. No. Turn around. You're blocking the entrance. Don't make this any more difficult than it needs to be. Step *away* from the gates."

"No, wait! Let me speak to God. God, it's Linda. It's me. Please. You don't understand. There's been a mistake. Oh, my

God. Let me in. Please let me in! I don't know what I've done wrong, but I don't want to go to hell. I won't like it there; I know I won't. I don't belong there. I am a good person. I know I should have turned to you before now, but I didn't. I'm sorry. I don't know why I didn't. Please let me in! Please, please let me in! God help me!"

I blinked my thoughts away, but they were quickly replaced with new ones that were equally ripe and horribly potent. I was terrified at the thought of not being able to talk to my mother on the phone again. I was terrified at the thought of not being able to see her old brown cardigan as I walked through customs. I was terrified at the prospect of the devil jabbing her up the arse with his trident. I was terrified of the possibility that my mother might become the center of the Lord's cosmic joke—the joke being that my mother had been good all her life but she wasn't a churchgoer and seldom spoke of matters of the soul. She was now fading away. She was confused and very stubborn. She thought aromatherapy was chemotherapy, and she was adamant that her veterinarian was coming to give her some new teeth. Her mind was breaking down. How was I going to get her to understand the looming peril her soul faced if she failed to "convert?"

My mother quietly clung to the remnants of her life, and I wandered about, wishing it was me. I would then look at my little children, glad that it wasn't. I hated myself for that.

When my son's teacher spoke to me, I would muster an insipid smile. "Charlie didn't hand his homework in on time, Mrs. Tirri."

"Oh." I'd replied.

I peeled the potatoes, fed the dogs, and put out the trash in a state of calm chaos. Only one thing dominated my thoughts: what God had in store for my mother's soul.

When my children were in school and my husband was safely out of the house, I would pour myself a glass of wine and reach for the remote. Using the television as their biggest medium, Christianity presented its God to me. Channel 372 and the stations around it broadcast our current monotheistic worldview. Airing around the clock, the modern representatives of Christianity make known the conditions of this reality. Appealing to believers like me, one station after another offers its teachings through the words of people like Betty and James Robison, John Hagee, Joyce Meyer, Bishop T. D. Jakes, Don Stewart, Joni Lamb, and Dr. Mark Charona. Kenneth and Gloria Copeland deliver Bible-based teachings, and Paula White is busy harvesting souls. Benny Hinn runs a ministry of singing and preaching as well as offering us testimonials and miraculous healing. Perry Stone can offer us a prophetic and practical study of God's word. Rod Parsley reveals what God has spoken to him. The Reverend Pat Robertson presents news buttressed with inspiration from God's word. Jesse Duplantis, Kirk Cameron, and Joel Osteen offer packed audiences their respective understanding of Christianity. Ed Young provides biblical instruction for living a Christian life. *Changing Your World* is hosted by Creflo and Taffi Dollar, and Billy Graham's Classic Crusades run for hours. Hal Lindsey's show, *International Intelligence Briefing*, brings insight to the news and how it relates to Bible prophesy. Bishop Eddie Long present information about the Holy Spirit, all shown on Christian television broadcast twenty-four hours a day, seven days a week.

I often reached for the Bible, but a cursory glance was all I could manage. I opened its pages at random, hoping that God's words would leap out and enlighten me. But I felt anything *but*; I just felt bemused, odd. I put the Holy Book back on my nightstand, remembering to dust it from time to time out of reverence for God's alleged word. I couldn't fathom it, but I still *respected* it. After putting my duster down, I would once again revisit my television set, prepared to trust the men and women who "got" God's plan for us in a way that I hadn't managed to.

I tried to soak in the comfort and love of God, but I was so at odds with Him placing a condition on my mother's redemption that I couldn't really manage that.

Was my mother saved?

I doubted it.

Was she honest, good, kind and moral?

Yes, she was! She most certainly was!

But according to the Christians, none of that matters. Who cares whether she was kind and good? If she didn't accept Jesus as her Lord and Savior, God would damn her.

Did God brush His hands together in a "that's that" gesture? Or were His fists hanging at His sides, clenched into balls? Or, was He simply shaking His head at a solemn St. Peter in exasperation at my mother's non-compliance?

"Hello Linda, God here. What can I say? I've given you many chances—*so* many chances. I have often thought, *Maybe today will be the day. Maybe today I can get Linda's attention.* Many people have crossed your path who could have helped you with what should have been a very simple procedure. Do you remember attending a dinner dance on that beautiful June evening in 1981? There was a lady there dressed in pearls and navy chiffon. She tried to speak to you about my Son. She spoke very kindly on the merits of turning your life over to Jesus, but all you did was offer her a cigarette and tell her how lovely her hair looked! What about that nice man who knocked on your front door one Sunday evening? He had a load of pamphlets concerning my Son's sacrifice that might have been a great deal of use to you. You assured him that you would read them, but after waving him goodbye, you just rolled them up, put them in the fireplace and set light to the kindling. You burned them! What about the time you had that lymphoma removed from your leg? The nurse with the curly auburn hair ever-so-casually talked about spiritual matters, but you just swallowed a painkiller and asked for another! *Why bother*!? I said to myself. *Why bloody bother?* What about the first time that you considered divorcing your children's father? I saw you walk into that little church on Broad street. I saw you sitting there in the front pew, crying over your deliberations. With a little tip off from me, that charming priest came out and tried to show you the light, but you just thought it was a shame that priests weren't allowed to marry and hoped you'd meet someone with eyes as gentle as his. You married Frank in a church. Did that not mean anything to you? Don't tell me that you got married in a church just so a lovely backdrop meant some nice photographs would grace your mantelpiece. Did you see the crucifixes? Did you see the Saints? Did you pay any attention to the words of the hymns that you sung in school? Did you pay attention to anything? What did you see, Linda? What did you see? Nothing, it seems—and I worked very hard in the hope that you would. Very hard. And now you have a lump the size of a grapefruit forcing itself against your brain. I suppose it's a little hard now to think straight, but you have had many chances, Linda. You really have. Let's face it. You have been alive for fifty-nine years, and you could have taken care of all this a long time ago. I've been sitting here year after year, drumming my fingers, and you never bothered to look this way. Not once. You completely ignored my call for salvation and foolishly chose not to recite a few simple words. This is not my fault. It's yours! Granted, to be hard-working, gentle and conciliatory was honorable, and you did very well at that. You were often meek, and although you will not inherit the earth, I admire your qualities, Linda. I really do. So does St. Peter. But virtue wasn't the key. I don't know where you got that idea! You missed the point. You were supposed to turn your life over to Jesus and believe that He died for your sins. It would have taken only five minutes to say the right words. I'm not greedy. Five minutes—that would have been enough. What's the big deal?"

What about the lady in the bed opposite my mother? She only had a few weeks to live. Maggie was a warm, chatty sort, kind and well-wishing. Was God going to let Maggie into heaven or was He going to rid Himself of her too? What about the nurses? Did they know how to get into God's good book? Should I tell them?

And what happens to all those who, as they grow into adults, don't see much of anything outside of themselves—let alone God? What if one is so bogged down with guilt, humiliation, or some horrible mental addiction that seeing God is only a distant prospect? What about all those who, after experiencing crappy childhoods, suddenly die in a car accident at the age of eighteen? What does their future hold? Do teenagers have a get-out clause? Can God be persuaded?

"No I can't. Stop whining. It's not my fault you were treated so badly. I didn't neglect you—your parents did. Don't take it out on me. And if you hadn't been going so fast on that motorbike, you would have had a little longer to get your act together. You should have gotten saved before you got your driver's license, young man. Accepting my only-begotten Son as Lord and Savior would have served you well. Now what's done is done. I'm busy. I have a lot on my plate."

My mother's life was almost over, and I had worked myself into a bit of a state. I wasn't eating much, and after admiring my new skinny frame, I would splash cold water over my puffy eyes and cry again.

It was time to leave for England. After grabbing some sunglasses, I humped my suitcase into my car and headed for the airport.

Once on board the transatlantic flight, I buckled my seatbelt and the First Officer informed the passengers of the flight details. I had a few *details* of my own to consider. Like how to secure the safety of mother's soul and score a place for her in heaven. If was just a question of flying a stupid jet across a pond, I could handle it—drunk *and* blindfolded! I ordered a drink, and then another. I needed to get trashed. I couldn't deal with it anymore. I drank myself into a blubbering mess, and the woman sitting next me moved to another seat. Eventually, I passed out, and hours later, I woke up at the top of decent, recovering from a dream of a menacing God surrounded by a load of smug angels. "Come on, Sarah," He had jeered. "It's shit-or-bust now, darling."

Christ, I felt awful, but I had to get my act together. I had to focus. My mother needed me. She was pretty mummy-like by this point. She had now lost all mobility and could barely speak, but I couldn't let that put me off. I had a mission to accomplish.

"I think I can, I think I can," I said to myself as I drove through the West Sussex countryside. But what if I couldn't? I wiped my sweaty palms on my jeans. I needed some backup. I needed to talk to a representative of God immediately. I didn't want an American evangelist, but an *English* go-between, a man of the cloth who dealt with the dying for a living. Subcontracting my mission was my only choice. The chaplain must take over now. Maybe *he* would be able to get my mother to talk to her maker. *He* was a professional; he had received the proper training; this was *his* turf. Maybe my mother wouldn't burn in

hell for all eternity after all. Maybe, just *maybe*, Father John of St. Barnabas's Hospice could turn things around. I kept my fingers crossed and pressed down on the accelerator. *"I hope he can, I hope he can."*

Father John ushered me into the same small tearoom where I had met with the doctor many times over the last couple of weeks, listening while he filled me in on the details of my mother's demise. I sat down in the familiar floral chair and leaned forward while I tried to explain my predicament to the jolly, very British chaplain. I told him of the Christians who believed that my mother's only road to salvation was to convert before she died. I explained that she might have actually done this, but that I couldn't be sure—there just wasn't an outward sign. She had never particularly mentioned God or Jesus, and I couldn't take any chances. It wasn't enough for me to hope she had talked to God. I needed her to know that she must...

The chaplain interrupted me. I looked into his eyes and tried to gauge his expression. At first I thought his manner was one of contention and irritation. I didn't say anything and waited patiently for his proper feelings of compassion to return. He then explained to me in no uncertain terms that God was *not* sitting up in heaven judging my mother. "God loves her; she is His creation and His child," he said to me.

I wanted to brush my mother's hair and massage lotion into her hands.

I wanted to tell that I loved her with all my heart.

I wanted to tell her that, although there had been many times that I had been terribly angry with her, I actually adored her.

I wanted to tell her funny stories of our trips around the world together.

I wanted to mention the words *Kuala Lumpur* and *turkey bacon* and watch her rock back with the force of her laughter.

I wanted to cry.

The day before my mother went into a coma, I saw her in a cage. I walked through the corridor of the hospice to meet with her big, brown, beautiful eyes, but she just stared straight ahead. She couldn't move. Her head was motionless. Her eyeballs were fixed and she was unable to blink.

The nurses had shifted my mother to one side of the bed. They rolled out huge Velcro straps and attached her to a hoist. Once the button was pushed, my mother's body doubled over into a kind of slouchy sitting position and she was slowly maneuvered through the air. The nurses chatted while she completed her journey, then they lowered her onto a seat—a seat with a hole in it. Various clips were attached to two-inch metal bars. This formed a kind of medical scaffolding that kept my mother from falling off the seat. The cage commandeered the new role of Linda's muscles, and huge rubber wheels supporting this contraption allowed my mother the privilege of experiencing her very last journey.

I heard water gushing from the taps in the germ-free bathroom and waited quietly while the nurses went about their daily program of keeping my mother clean. With a *kill-the-bitch-kill-the-bitch* fervor, the tumor had finally accomplished the first step of what it had set out to do. It had paralyzed her entire body, every last millimeter of it.

When the bathroom ordeal was over, my mother slept soundly, and I walked out of St. Barnabas' Hospice and lit a cigarette. I blew God a smoke ring and wondered what the hell He was thinking.

The following day, my brother and I signed the visitors' registry and walked through the double doors into our mother's ward for the last time. I still don't know whether our mother heard us coming or sensed us coming, but she had somehow managed to lift her chin. Our mother, who had been *completely* paralyzed, who hadn't been able to move *any* of her muscles, needed to tell us something. Mark and I stood still and watched as our mother's eyes met ours. I saw her lips move very slowly. She then gave us this small, death-defying smile—the most beautiful smile I had ever seen. She needed to tell her children that she was doing just fine, and I knew she was going to be fine because I could read her smile. I had always been able to do that.

Something had happened while she had been sleeping. She knew something that I didn't. My mother wasn't going to hell. She knew that she had found peace, peace she had been searching for all her life, and it wasn't frightening for her anymore.

My mother looked at her children one last time, then lowered her eyelids. The lovely Linda didn't wake up again, and her body died a few days later. And a few days after that, my mother's coffin was lowered into its final resting place. The weather was beautiful, the flowers looked magnificent, and my family mourned.

CHAPTER THREE

The End Times

More recently, another bout of End Times rhetoric began constricting the psyches of those who actually believe *the end of the world as we know it* is upon us. This happened after 9/11, and now as a result of the COVID-19 pandemic, the representatives of Christianity are at it again...

God's anger was the subject of another sermon I witnessed on television. It was delivered by a portly preacher from Texas. This preacher has a commanding presence and his ministry owns a multimillion-dollar auditorium masquerading as a church. He has a massive following and has committed masses of biblical scripture to memory so it rolls off his tongue with eloquence and sting. Bible in one hand, fear in the other, he fervently proclaimed, "The purpose of God's wrath is to demonstrate His hatred of sin." I felt the rhythm of the music from *The Omen* as I heard him preach about the anti-Christ. He screamed something about a proclamation: A third of humanity would apparently be annihilated. There would be global food shortages as a result of the entire animal kingdom being wiped out. Fuck that! I thought as I switched the channel to a cooking show on The Food Network. As I watched the host form a burger patty, I wondered something: Is it the fearful aspects of Christianity that provoke such zeal from all those evangelists who sincerely believe it's *their* mission to wake up the rest of us? They must evangelize. They *must* preach, for they are duty-bound to let us know to what *their* God intends!

What *does* their God intend?

Well, for anyone whose knowledge of Christianity's prediction of the End Times is vague, know this: If you're not on God's A-list (saved) at the time He chooses to wreak havoc, your life will become your worst nightmare.

And if any of my readers are not familiar with Christianity's "rapture prediction" or don't feel that they are "rapture-ready," know that it's really quite simple—God is going to "beam up" the saved. All those who get left behind will witness a cosmic abduction. Literally, in the blink of an eye, we are told to expect the disappearance of millions of people.

The logistics of Christianity's alleged Rapture caused me a fair bit of concern. On more than one occasion I have drained the pasta while indulging in this odd grisly reverie: What if, when God raptures us, He snatches the cockpit crew from a British Airways night flight from Heathrow to JFK and whisks them off to heaven while the plane is still airborne? I was once a stewardess for BA; I know what goes on. Who's gonna to land the plane? Should the cabin crew in these End Times possess a commercial pilot's license, just in case?

What if God raptures both the anesthetist *and* the surgeon while Nancy Jenkins is undergoing open heart surgery? Do we have a God who doesn't give a damn about Nancy because she wasn't saved, and as far as He is concerned, she can bleed to death?

What if an exhausted family of four are driving back from Typhoon Lagoon and God decides to rapture all but the lady snoozing in the passenger seat? Will she find herself speeding along Interstate 4 at seventy miles per hour with no driver? Will God have *already* raptured the people in the oncoming vehicles so the carnage that prevails *only* involves those who don't believe the Christian doctrine?

"Hello everyone, your monotheistic God here. Let me reveal to you something about myself. During the Old Testament days, I suffered from what you presently refer to as bipolar disorder. Christianity then came along and, through the New Testament's version of Me, told you that I made an attempt to improve. I acknowledged my own shortcomings and wanted to be a good God again. But here we are, 2,000 years down the line, and my Old Testament routine is about to grip the world with a vengeance. I did try, you know! I plan to come as a thief in the night. I plan to rapture a large number of you—call it celestial selection if you like. I am going to do this because I am a little picky about who will join me and who won't. But being the benevolent, loving God that I am, I will make it very clear as to what it takes to please me: If you're saved, you're in; if you're not saved, you're out. And if you're out—it's show time! Some of you refer to My cosmic eruption as the Apocalypse, and some of you call it the End of Days, but frankly I don't care what you call it. I am creator of the Goddamn universe, for crying out loud; I've got bigger fish to fry."

Apart from a few stable animals, the odd family member, and a few well-dressed men, Jesus' first entry into this world went relatively unnoticed. According to the Christians, His second one won't be. Many believe that Jesus, as He embarks on His second coming, is going to be surrounded by white horses, shrouded in a blaze of glory.

"Hi God, Sarah here. I don't believe Jesus is going to revisit us physically from the heavens riding amidst a herd of white horses accompanied by all those who you raptured. I did believe this once. I don't now. And I don't believe Jesus died for my sins, so I am apparently going to be left behind. If this is the case, can you do me a favor? Can you personally prepare Jesus' flight plan? Can you please see to it that, as He makes his way towards the Mount of Olives, he wafts right over my house? Kindly warn me, so I can put my dogs in the garage. I have a fabulous new camera, and getting the picture of Jesus riding white stallions over the rooftops accompanied by a host of angels and saints would be great for my Instagram. I'm pretty sure that *The National Enquirer* would pay me handsomely for it. Last week it said, "Aging actress gives birth to reptilian baby." The week before it said, "Mermaid found off the coast of Seattle." Next week it could say, "Jesus steals Santa Claus' sleigh." I'd really appreciate that. Thanks a lot."

The luminaries of our monotheistic/Christian culture believe Jesus died for their sins. The premise of their existence is based on the notion that (praise the Lord) one can escape God's fury by believing Christianity's doctrine of atonement. Joyce Meyer believes that she'll get to heaven because she is *saved* from the potential *wrath* of the God, whom she *worships*. Excuse me while I scratch my head! But what galls me most is the selfishness that is automatically associated with this worldview. Does Joyce Meyer actually believe she is saved with an *I'm all right, Jack* mentality lurking in the recesses of her mind, likening her personal victory to a rat deserting a sinking ship? I don't know. I love Joyce—she has helped me through a lot of dogging mindsets—but the thought of her expounding such beliefs with what she might consider to be a clean conscience, leaves me cold. If I die tomorrow—unsaved and condemned—Joyce Meyer and her Christian counterparts might exude benevolence over the terrifying fate of my soul. But if their beliefs are picked apart and couched in terms that better disclose the truth, nothing more than a *you had your chance and you blew it* mentality would reveal itself. Anyone who preaches spirituality from the perspective that God is going to "save some and harm the rest" really shouldn't be preaching at all. They should be on their knees praying that their personal veil of fear be lifted so they can see that God is love, and Christianity preaches the antithesis of it.

Now, in the light of my previous statement, some, with a burning indignation, might quickly insist that anyone who is interested can easily learn that, according to biblical doctrine, "God's favor" is a "free gift" offered to "whosoever will." Rather than prompting disgust towards Christianity or monotheistic religions in general, this section is apt to bring into question the integrity of the writer. But if you find yourself questioning *my* integrity, let me ask *you* something: How can you possibly believe—with *any* integrity—in a God who offers "favor" as a "free gift" to "whosoever will" The idea of a separate God who dangles a carrot and fucks with those who, for some reason, fail to grasp it is abhorrent to me.

And besides, if Christianity is the "truth," why have so many people not responded to it. Why has the human experience been so discordant over the last two thousand years? A Christian might answer this question by saying that our troubled history is due to Christian perfection not being achieved. One might then deduce that *time* is all that is needed for man to vindicate himself—ushering in a new age of purity. But I would hasten to point out that appealing to the future for the fulfillment of Christian perfection is the only justification Christianity has left for defending its existence. But we are also told that the future is carved in stone and most of us will be unable to make positive use of whatever time is left. God has had enough! All bets are off! Time's up! Most of us have misused our free will, and the world is full of the result—sin. So, it would seem that the *time*

25

argument contradicts the argument that the world is in fact beyond redemption without the Apocalypse to sweep it all clean.

In fact, most Christians believe this world is spoiled by sin, and that what we see going on around us has nothing to do with God's design, but rather, man's dissension. *"It's not Gods fault, Mrs. Tirri. It's ours. God didn't design this world to be what it is. We strayed from the path of righteousness."* God, we are told, is fed up with it all now, and plans to judge us and restore the earth to what He originally intended before that bitch Eve took a bite from an apple. God Himself is now ready to step in and purify everything supernaturally, sanitize the world. A little housekeeping is all that's needed. Apparently, we've failed to get it on more than one occasion, and just like the good old days when God drowned us in the Genesis flood, He is planning once again to cleanse the earth. God is going to use the entire force of nature to do this. He is going to burn all the grass and one third of the trees. He will turn oceans into blood and send down hails of fire. He will kill the sea creatures and sink the ships that are sailing about. He will dry up our rivers and springs and contaminate what water remains. He'll mess with the sun so we don't get much light, and then, He'll restore it so we all get scorched. God will release lightning and earthquakes and cause the volcanoes to erupt. And, listen to this one: He'll release huge swarms of locusts not to kill us, just to torment us. Hallowed be Thy Name! He'll cause loathsome sores and He will at some point plunge us into total darkness. All the angels will be whooping with delight, because God extracting His vengeance upon the wicked is the highlight of the millennia.

The monotheistic/Christian preachers and authors seem to be (perhaps unwittingly) doing their best to bring the said End

Times about—and the sooner the better. In their attempts to forecast the future, they study ancient mythology—trying to make sense of it through an excruciating analytical process. The Book of Revelations is picked apart and pieced back together. A fictional, terrifying prophecy is then sold as the true future of humanity and millions believe it. The Western world needs to make sure it's got the right God. Listen to popular Christian "prophesy," and you too might begin to wonder whether we have.

John the Divine (fabulous name) wrote the prophetic Book that freaks us all out. He told the world that Jesus personally sent him an angel… *"Hi John the Divine, I am an angel, a monotheistic messenger, and I come before you to bring you the good news. We are all a little busy up here, so God has appointed you the role as Grim Reaper. The Book of Revelation is your baby. It's a shit job, but someone's got to do it."*

What an ordeal that must have been! If I stepped out of my front door and "saw" seven golden lamp stands cloaking a chap who wore a gold belt around his chest with a sword coming out of his mouth, I would be pretty freaked out even if he did appear friendly. How did John the Divine react, I wonder? Did fear ever permeate his imagination?

How *can* forming dire projections of the future based on the hallucinations of some 2,000-year-old hermit be that useful? The Western world inherited an apocalyptic theory of the End Times from a semiliterate fanatical culture. This patriarchal, superstitious, adrenaline-governed society was endemic to the lands surrounding the Mediterranean—yet this is where our spiritual beliefs originate. Trying to understand what our future holds based on some ancient paranoia is something we should stop doing. We have evolved. We are an advanced race; we don't need to be thinking like a man who couldn't identify the origins of thunder.

"Don't be daft; the forecasts in the Bible are not actually going to happen," I hear many of you declare. "It's all just a load of mythology that the impressionable believe is factual!" Well, if this is something you at one time or another have also thought, know this: The premise of your one-life-could-be-a-bitch existence comes from the religions that believe all this bunkum about beasts and their attendant mayhem *will* actually happen. The source of the Western world's current beliefs concerning the nature of this reality (monotheism) came largely from the religions that actually believe that the "beast" could be a monster in the literal sense, a demonic force infiltrating our minds, or he could be a real man who will reveal himself as the anti-Christ in an attempt to take over the world!

Acharya S, in her book *The Christ Conspiracy, The Greatest Story Ever Sold,* says, "Another biblical 'code' in need of decipherment is the Book of Revelation, which has mystified and fascinated people for centuries with its bizarre imagery and purported prophecy. This fascination has led to endless speculation and interpretation of its 'prophecy' by biblical literalists, who, being unable to do anything else with it, usually interpret revelation allegorically. Needless to say, despite centuries of attempts to decode the text and to associate its players with a variety of world leaders, nations and organizations, Revelation remains a mystery because it is, in fact, not prophecy, and its drama does not take place on earth."

I have a Bible that is probably one of many with the title "Good News," although much of what it contains sounds like anything *but* good news to me. The introductory paragraph to the Book of Revelation says this: "For the most part the book consists of several series of revelations and visions presented in symbolic language that would have been understood by Christians of that day, but would have remained a mystery to all others."

We *are* the "all others," and while our present understanding of the word prophecy exists, the mystery will remain *just that*— for prophecy cannot be validated until it has been fulfilled. It is *only* the fulfillment of it that will enable us to reminisce over the biblical drama that made no sense and recognize the symbolism for what it actually meant. But having said that, I believe a more accurate understanding of the true nature of prophecy will arise as our spiritual worldview evolves. Prophecy is not what we think. (I talk more about this later.)

Is the truth behind the apocalyptic revelation really this? "And there was a battle in heaven; Michael and his angels battled with the dragon, and the dragon fought his angels. And the dragon fought with his enemy. And they did not prevail; neither was their place found any more in heaven. And that great dragon was cast down, the ancient serpent, he who is called the devil and Satan, who leads astray the whole world...." Listen, sweetie, there's only one thing that leads the whole world astray, and that's the monotheistic illusion. Maybe monotheism is the metaphoric great dragon. Maybe all those who saw the future actually saw the demise of the religions that uphold it, not the demise of the world. And the rage that was to pervade the earth was the residual fury of monotheistic religion clinging to its reign, thrashing about as it watched humanity free itself.

I believe it is the bogus teachings of our monotheistic religions that have caused many to become atheists. My brother is an atheist, a devout one, and some time ago I asked him what he saw for humanity's future. He said, "Forget it Sarah. Try to enjoy life under the guise of the primal instincts that have no greater meaning than randomly making more of us. The future is not worth worrying about. We will rot when we die, and until then, it's dog eat dog, and if we're full, dog *hump* dog."

My brother might not realize it, but he fell for the Western premise of a life without hope. The average atheist shuns religion and opts for mechanistic science's version of reality, which tells us that what we experience here is just an arbitrary manifestation of chance happenings. My brother doesn't *believe* that the world will get better, because he doesn't believe a bigger picture exists.

But I have faith that there is a bigger picture, and the fact that many of us are looking around and wondering *Is this the Best God could do?* means that we haven't understood *what* that bigger picture is. I believe there *has* to be hope: Why would a loving God have bothered setting up this whole world, knowing that what much of humanity ultimately faced would be fearful and humiliating? I doubt whether He's pleased with Christianity's doomsayers using their abortive position to diminish the magnitude of what He did, and He is probably not all that happy with the scientific conception of randomness either.

I believe it is crucial that we do "get it," or we'll face the implications of not getting it. And thinking ones thoughts into a reality, I believe, is very easily done. If we think thoughts of doom and destruction, there's a good chance that what were once "mere" thoughts will become real.

Humanity must project a good outcome; projecting a good outcome is the building block to creating a better world. Hope is the pathway to enlightenment, because when we come to terms with the enormity of the reality in which we dwell, we will be able to understand *how* to consciously create all that we hope for.

In fact, my metaphysical and philosophical intuition tells me that hope is something humanity must have, something we cannot possibly live without. Hope is the culmination of our evolution. Hope is the ability to be able to look at the future as magnificent potential, to marvel rather than shudder with dismal doom. Hope is creative, and the lack of it depletive. Hope is not a commodity on which much of the Western world dwells, however. Read Revelation. Listen to the fear-forecasters. We are all supposedly facing some sort of doomsday as prophesied by the man-made notion of bleakness. The proponents of Christianity would like us to believe there is ultimately no hope that we will ever solve our own problems, but this illusion of hopelessness causes fear, and there are some who have a harder time dealing with their fear than others. We should sidestep these people, for they form their fearful conclusions and project them onto the rest of us, compounding *our* fears by preaching hopelessness. A *crappy ending* is not what God designed, but you might have noticed that many of those who forecast doom and gloom *profit* from it. We should stop listening to fear-forecasters who tell us that cosmic chaos will take over the world and that we should get "saved." We should stop listening to the fear-forecasters who tell us that we won't have to endure anything because we won't be able to think straight as the radiation slowly poisons our cells. We should stop listening to the fear-forecasters who tell us that some sort of "bubonic" virus is airborne and will infect all those not wearing a mask (Buy two get one free). We should stop listening to the fear-forecasters who tell us that the War on Terror will eventually threaten our children's safety, the fear-forecasters who advocate *more* security and *more* restriction. If our hope dwindles to near depletion, we might well hand over the reins to our governing bodies, which will make decisions without restraint because the rest of us are now busy preparing ourselves for the worst and might not particularly care.

What we are dealing with are mass proclamations of fear conjured in the imaginations of the influential. Now don't get me wrong. There is nothing *wrong* with using our imaginations, because imagination is the mechanism by which we create what will happen to us. But in our mainstream Western culture we have yet to hear of the earthly joys and splendor that await us— joys and splendor that a God who loves us would have surely included in the blueprint. Is there any religion in the West that doesn't sell us fearful predictions and then sit back and watch us create them? Are there any ecologists who predict anything other than global warming creating outrageous cancers and the need for a massive shield over the parts of the world that can afford it? Are there any philosophies, stories, ideas, new information, or scenarios that start with: All is well, the future looks great?

Is God (the real God) *itching* to say something like?

"Hello, God here. The future looks great, and despite what you might have believed previously, all is well. The stranglehold with which the Western religions of fear have gripped humanity is almost over. You are evolving, and you will become stronger. Through self-realization you will see more clearly. The outcome of your planet's evolution is glorious. It is a sure thing. I designed a much bigger reality than the monotheistic religions purport, and you are about to discover it. Stop listening to anyone who predicts anything other than a hopeful outcome, because this type of preaching has nothing to do with your future, nothing to do with the truth, and it certainly has nothing to do with me. What I designed is nothing other than first-rate magnificence made manifest, and anyone who tells you otherwise is simply serving his own interests. A separate God will not afflict you with terror or attempt to separate and cleanse you. If you continue poisoning your home, the planet might do what it needs to in order to protect itself, but it's also quite forgiving and can mend. The future's good—very good. You must get this You will reach your goal. It cannot be any other way because this is the underlying truth of your evolution. Evolution was not an experiment, a test with right or wrong answers with a big downside for screwing up—I wouldn't have done that to you. What you intend becomes reality, but this little esoteric piece of information never got aired. You must consciously create the future as positive and have faith that the outcome of your beliefs will indeed be your future. Your future is being believed into a reality as I speak. I designed it this way. You must now consciously guide what you believe, making sure your beliefs have nothing to do with the second-rate nonsense the monotheistic religions spew forth. Start to question the monotheistic God so you can find some sort of truth. Truth is to be found in this way, because truth comes from seeking My bigness, not from absorbing the viewpoint that I have a multitude of lower impulses and you are at the mercy of them. I am so very sorry that this master religion still gets your attention. Stop following the Pied Piper. You have no use for him now."

The End Time is in fact real. We *are* living in the End Time—the end of the monotheistic reign. A new age is upon us, and this means dispelling a manmade God and every belief that opposes magnificence and labeling it a process of evolutionary expansion. Dispelling limiting beliefs is the evolutionary process at work. It is through dispelling limiting beliefs that primitive man evolves into civilized man.

The potential of humanity to rise up to its magnificence depends on how we interpret God; to understand God is to understand ourselves, and once we understand who we are, the way we perceive life changes. It is our distorted perceptions of what God actually did that causes the dysfunction that humanity has become rather used to. The madness of this world is simply a murky expression of religious distortion—false notions of God and the reality He created.

The "big God–little human" worldview and the implications of not seeing the truth, I believe, is causing a lot of problems. I also believe that any seeker—Jew, Christian or Muslim (the Big Three)—who wants to know the larger truth won't find it in the monotheistic premise. They might find a lot of things, fearful things, just like I did, but only partial truth. A partial truth is better than no truth, of course, but we need the whole truth now because the conditions of this world won't improve without it.

If the doctrines of the Big Three made complete sense and the world was good, we could assume that what the monotheistic religions offered us as spiritual teaching was the truth. But this is simply not the case. The world is chaotic and full of misery, and—excuse my presumptuousness—perhaps it's the phony monotheistic premise of reality that has contributed largely to this.

How is it that the monotheistic worldview has prevailed for so long? I've asked myself this question many times since my mother's death, and I'm still not sure of the answer. Perhaps man has a soft spot for tradition, a sentimental weakness of some sort. Perhaps it was the Inquisitions of the Middle Ages that *tempted* us to accept the monotheistic premise of human smallness—to think differently for hundreds of years meant persecution and so we stopped doing that.

Some readers might consider the teachings of Christianity to be fearful, freaky, laughable even; but what's *not* so laughable is the fact that the Western world has *premised* its *existence* on the monotheistic idea of reality. What is the premise of our existence? We basically handed this spiritual question over to the Christians and blindly accepted their authority regarding the reality in which we find ourselves. And as for the rest of us? We might not believe in the doctrines of Judaism, Christianity or Islam, but nevertheless, most of us in the West mistakenly believe we get one random life. And because *monotheistic* spirituality and mechanistic science holds a monopoly in the Western world, many overlook the fact that "reality" is a great deal bigger than one might have thought. Although the atheists, free thinkers, and skeptics might dismiss the beliefs of the Big Three with an intolerant flip of the hand, it *should* be acknowledged that monotheism provided *the premise* upon which our miserly view of "reality" was formulated. The Western world needs to know more than we have believed *from* the Christian church or ignored *because* of the Christian church.

How the Western world came to accept the monotheistic worldview might forever be a subject for historians to weigh, and perhaps laymen do not need to get too bogged down with pondering the historical ins-and-outs, but it is my firm conviction that holding on to the traditional one-life-could-be-a-bitch-and-we-are-all-in-need-of-saving premise as defined for us by Christianity and not finding a replacement, will mean that God's (bigger) plan for us all will remain hidden.

For a very long time now, and with few exceptions, the common man of the West has lived in complete ignorance of his purpose here, and centuries of stalling within the confines of the second-rate premise bequeathed us by monotheism has caused us a great deal of suffering. Learning, what could be termed, the hard way didn't mean we wouldn't evolve of course; it just meant for many a mediocre fragmented reality would feature heavily on the program.

In the following chapter, I speak of my Aunty Joan—my mentor—*my angel* —a Christian. Aunty Joan was the finest person I have *ever* known; she is now sharing recipes with Mother Teresa in a heaven that is rightfully hers. She lived a Christian life. She was always open to giving and loving but I believe was secretly plagued by bouts of futility and unanswered questions. She simply "got" the wrong God. I know this now. But the fact that she was willing to *try* to understand the bigger picture was a benefit to everyone who came near her.

As I am writing this chapter, I am listening to a radio commercial. The man currently speaking is selling accelerated masters degrees at a private university in Florida. His opening pitch is that he wants to live his life by *Christian principles*. I didn't hear too much more of what he said because I was too busy wondering what Christian principles are as opposed to regular principles. Like *my angel*, I know I aspire to be helpful, truthful, kind, fair, friendly, supportive, loyal, faithful, noble, trustworthy, cooperative, decent, gracious, dignified, compassionate, righteous, generous, and magnanimous. In fact, I can think of a much longer list of principles that I am hoping to embody as I live my life, but I am *not* a Christian. *"No shit, Sarah,"* I hear some of you proclaim at the top of your lungs!

When I was building my house, my housekeeper-to-be pulled up one day as I was discussing something with the contractor. She wasn't looking for domestic employment at that point, but asked whether I wanted to buy some silk flower arrangements that she was making. Her introduction opened with a smile and a confident reassurance that she was trustworthy because, as she put it, "I am a good Christian lady." She *is* a good Christian lady, and I employed her and I love her, but she is not good *because* she is a Christian—she is good due to a whole assortment of reasons that have nothing to do with her religious orientation.

Another friend and I were discussing my antipathy towards Christianity, and she said to me, "I had no idea of the doctrines of Christianity. You are my first real exposure to it all, and I agree with ninety-five percent of what you say. I am shocked. I have *always* believed that I was a Christian."

Why is being good these days synonymous with being a Christian? How did that happen?

I have met *many* decent, kind "Christians" (good people) throughout my life. Seemingly, they chose to respect the primary tenets of Christianity and questions of its credibility didn't arise for them. Others, like my angel, decided to endure life with a stoic acceptance and a nagging discontent that took one into the blessed afterlife. Other clever folks decided five-sense scientific conformation was the only way truth could be validated, which is utter lunacy when you consider the magnitude of God's design. Others, like me, questioned Christianity and got labeled anarchists. Others shunned the traditional religious premise, refusing to come up with an alternative, and wrestled with the psychological disarray associated with its materialistic replacement.

All the time we submerge ourselves in the hugely-magnified material reality belonging to a world that was simply trying to recover from spiritual distortion, we must remember that we are doing this because we have lost the bigger picture. Traditional science and our monotheistic religions—Judaism, Christianity and Islam—will not explain the *magnitude* of this existence to us, so it might be that each of us decides to expand his or her personal horizon. We might do this now or in ten years' time, but considering all the messed-up things that are going on in the world, we might not want to wait that long. Alternatively, we might choose to poodle along, accepting the watered-down version of reality that's broadcast from our television screens twenty-four hours a day, seven days a week, 365 days a year, failing on all counts to consider what a superficial path we're being led down.

The spiritual path of the West is now turning in ever-decreasing circles. It's time to get off and find another. The Western world must re-establish a spiritual balance, making us the well-rounded super species that we're destined to be. It's time the Western world explore other spiritual ideas and then our greatness *will* become the world's biggest example of what it means to have "got it."

We must understand what we're doing here. We have reached an evolutionary point at which nothing else is an option. Finding the true premise of our existence will enable us to automatically shed the shackles of limitation that keep us small. And it's about time that our bigness—and *not* the religious realms that divert us from it—becomes our focus. We've been evolving in a limited version of reality fostered by monotheistic religion, Judaism, Islam, and Christianity, which has profited very nicely from this affliction. As a result, we've developed limited beliefs concerning who we are. We are a *lot* bigger than we've been told, and so is the God that created us. A new premise of human magnitude will replace our current premise of human smallness, of that I am certain. But for the duration of the time we are tentative about our future and fail to establish a new spiritual premise as the basis for human existence, we'll continue to watch what goes on in the world and continue to think, *Is this the best God could do?*

Although the monotheistic religions I speak of are Middle Eastern in origin, they spread to the West and infected us all. The following chapters outline the Western doctrine of smallness. Throughout this book I refer to the creators of the Western premise using the following terms, which I use interchangeably:

the Western church
organized religion
Western religion
monotheistic religion monotheism
Judaism and Christianity and Islam
the Big Three

Apart from a smokescreen of different observances and tedious nitpicking of scriptural interpretation, their premise is basically the same: big God-little human. Christianity, like Judaism and Islam, is made up of many splinter groups. We all know them as: The Church of England, Roman Catholicism and its breakaway factions. We have the Protestants, the Lutherans, the Methodists, the Pentecostals, the Seventh Day Adventists, the Presbyterians, the Episcopalians, and the Baptists, to name but a few. Their cause is the same—to maintain their version of dogma that keeps us small. They've kept God's "plan" small too, but there comes a point at which *every* distortion *ever* told gets exposed, and that's because the evolution of mankind depends on its revelation.

Read on. I am peeling an onion here. I intend to bear out my claim that the monotheistic view of reality is belittling to an intelligent species, and you will come to see *how* I arrived at such an iconoclastic conclusion.

CHAPTER FOUR

The Pied Piper

Any resemblance between my childhood exposure to Christianity and that of the average American youth is purely coincidental. Things were different in 1970s England, very different, especially Sundays. I grew up in a land where the "Sunday experience" was restricted, to say the least. I hear things are a little different now—England has become more Americanized, thank God—but when I was a ten-year-old girl, all retail businesses in the country were denied permission to trade. The one exception was the sale of religion, of course. This marketing ploy, the best I have ever seen, ensured that on Sundays, everything *but* religion came to a grinding halt. The odd corner store might have been given a two-hour exception, but apart from that, there was more action on the Mary Celeste. Moreover, there were three channels on our television, and religion infiltrated all of them. The choice was pretty clear: Sundays meant boredom or religion.

In fact, boredom birthed many a captive audience. A surefire way for the Church to bring in the bread was to force everyone in the country to tolerate a day of rest under the guise of honoring the good Lord, who too rested on the seventh day. St. Mary's, St. Paul's, and St. Peter's all cashed in, for once we all appeared in church, whether out of boredom or actual respect, we could please the good Lord further by coughing up some cash when the velvet purse was passed around. Christianity was the only diversion on Sunday, and as a child, that was fine by me.

On many a Sunday, I trotted off with my friend to a church that held an hour-long retreat for the kids who would only have annoyed the adults if a provision hadn't been made for their containment. Congregants of all ages started out together, but after about twenty minutes, the children gladly left their parents and the adults gladly repositioned themselves to take full advantage of the extra room, smug in the knowledge that some other idiot had agreed to take on the responsibility of teaching their darling children what the hell it was that God wanted them to know.

Based upon their ages, the children joined their respective Sunday School groups—the Climbers, the Explorers, or the Pathfinders. The Climbers included kids who had only recently learned to do just that, climb. The Explorers was a group tailored for the average kindergartner who knew nothing of the world other than the diversion of seeing thirty other confused children hearing the same weird stuff about a baby who was born in a stable next to a pile of donkey ca-ca. Not an ordinary baby, a *special* baby, a baby whose majesty gave birth to a multibillion-dollar toy industry that allowed the Western world to indulge in a yearly celebration of gift-giving that got all us children hooked. The birth of Jesus insured that, once a year, we kids would be given a whole bunch of presents to celebrate His entry into this world. I loved Jesus. I thought He was great. The Christmas pardon from school meant presents, brightly colored ribbon, sparkling tree lights, merry-on-sherry adults, and better food and television shows than usual. I enjoyed another two-week vacation at Easter. At this time, I was given a big, creamy, chocolate egg, which apparently celebrated Jesus' exit from this world. Jesus ruled! And as a child, Christianity was fine by me.

Some might argue that there is nothing in biblical Christianity that suggests that Jesus Christ was born on December 25th, or on any other particular date for that matter. Nor does biblical Christianity suggest that anyone observe the day of his birth in any fashion whatsoever. However, it is my belief that these traditions are accepted by most as being of Christian origin. For me, the observance of this day started in childhood. I played the Virgin Mary when I was ten years old, and was furious over the fact that Mary didn't have any lines. The scenery shook, Joseph got a wedgie, and the Angel Gabriel burst into tears, but nevertheless, despite the distractions, I *believed* I was partaking in a Christian tradition. If someone had asked me what was unique about December the 25th, I would have said this was the day that a mute lady gave birth to a special baby. I would have said this because the Christian culture I grew up in had taught me this.

I went to Sunday School with my friend Georgina. Georgina would often look down her upper-middleclass nose at me, which she used to pick a lot as well. She went to Sunday School because her parents thought it was the proper thing for an upper-middleclass family to force upon their children. I went because I would have been bored otherwise. Our Sunday School group was called the Pathfinders. I cannot recollect much about the goings-on there. Only that it was an hour-long diversion of puzzling instruction that held boredom at bay. If ever I mentioned to my mother that I was bored, she would swiftly adopt a haughty stance and say things like, *"If you're bored Sarah, go and tidy your bedroom or start a butterfly collection. That's what I did when I was a little girl. I had lots of hobbies, and I was never bored. I collected wild flowers. I knew their Latin names."* Whereupon I would groan and opt for Church, for it beat the hell out of trapping butterflies or searching for the rare pale pink variety of Rose Bay Willow Herb. Besides, I enjoyed people-watching, and I genuinely liked the pomp and ceremony of church too. I loved singing *Onward Christian Soldiers* and *Oh Jesus I have Promised*, and I loved lighting the candles. One time, I actually contemplated *stealing* a silver candelabra and giving it to my mother for Mother's Day. But the Virgin Mary stared down at me from her stained-glass window, reminding me that my mother would be delighted to receive wild flowers again this year and that the candelabra belonged to God and was for us all to share.

I was baptized Roman Catholic, and the party-line was to adopt a disposition of reverence for the good Lord based on fear. If this was done successfully, a heavenly spot was for the taking. The Roman Catholic faction of Christianity offered me a load of God-pleasing, rigid rules and regulations, all of which I had broken many times. Repentance was then necessary to absolve me of my sins before I once again repeated the cycle.

Draped on the hill behind my house was an imposing medieval Roman Catholic Church. It was a particular favorite of mine and easy to get to. My friends and I would often aggravate the middle classes by following them into church and hogging the isle seats. We were there to pad our day by watching Father Francis carry out the two-hour-long service of ritual and reverence. While soaking up their arcane tones of veneration, the Roman Catholic service propelled me into a peculiar world of ceremonial worship, a different world, an ancient world. I watched it all, taking comfort in the knowledge that I could open the doors at any time and find myself back in the modern one.

Upon reentering the year 1977, my friends and I would head off to the adjacent tearoom. The ladies patrolling the tearoom gave away hot chocolate and cookies—not ordinary cookies but nice cookies, assorted cookies that my mother couldn't afford. The only drawback to scoffing ten cream-filled cookies was that we had to sit through the Roman Catholic rendition of what it meant to please God. I felt completely unmoved by what I heard. Maybe I was unmoved because I was a child, who knows? But what I *do* know is that the cream-filled cookies made it all worth it, and as I picked the chocolate chips out of my teeth, Christianity was fine by me.

Just as my teenage years loomed, my mother decided that we should up-sticks and experience something *more* in life. She was bored. I suppose I should have told her to start a butterfly collection, but I didn't, so our house was quickly sold, and we headed off to our new home—a quaint little terraced cottage hundreds of miles away in the market town of Honiton.

My mother's emotional volatility meant that she was eager to search for a new man and make him her husband. Number three—quickly found but short-lived—lasted about nine weeks, and after this marriage was annulled, she was soon looking for a replacement. Her fourth husband happened to be a wealthy man with a big house and an acute bipolar disorder. His name was Roy. After stuffing our possessions into black bin liners, we left our cottage and moved further up the high street to embark on a grander life of lunacy.

I didn't care about the change in our lifestyle. I was just tired of watching my mother make the same old mistakes, and she was tired of the look in my eyes that told her that this time I would not grin and bear it. My brother, being a little easier to tame, stayed behind, but I bolted. At the age of fourteen, I was fostered by a lovely lady named Rebecca. I lived with Rebecca until I was no longer welcome, and then I went off to Somerset to live with her mother, who was a devout Christian. Her name was Joan Elks—*my angel* —and I called her Aunty. Aunty Joan and I spent many Sunday evenings together attending an English church in the country village of Yarlington. I didn't mind going to church. I was just pleased my angel wanted me with her at a time when no one else seemed to.

The Church of St. Mary the Virgin in the parish of Camelot offered me weekly exposure to the more rural intricacies of impressing the good Lord. The country dwellers of Camelot comprised a congregation that varied in size depending on the outside temperature. If it was cold, the numbers would be fewer. God himself had apparently experienced painful arthritic joints brought on by the English climate, and it seemed the elderly were occasionally given the right to veto, without finding themselves in the time-out chair.

The congregation of St. Mary's would sit uncomfortably on the wooden pews, sharing a common thought: *I must have paid for these damn wooden benches to be upholstered a hundred times over.* We kept our backs straight and recited the Lord's Prayer. We were then required to spend twenty minutes on our knees. This was not as bad as it sounds. Plump prayer mats provided cushioning. As long as we were on our knees, we were told that God quite approved of us doing it comfortably.

After straightening our backs, we enjoyed a new position while listening to a couple of ambiguous passages read from the Bible by senior congregation members, who found the small print, let alone the content, difficult to fathom. And then we all sang a nice, long, unrecognizable hymn. I really liked the singing part, but only if I knew the words. I used to memorize the words and leave my hymnbook on the bench while singing loudly with my head held high. I got a kick out of being one of the few who didn't find it necessary to use a hymnbook, and I hoped that the rest of the congregation saw what a good little Christian I was. I routinely tested my religious agility by memorizing the doctrine too, giving myself marks out of ten for doing so.

After we had exercised our appalling voices, Holy Communion was given to all those who wanted to make a further contribution to God's happiness. I was always pissed off by the fact that I was not encouraged to take Holy Communion, a ritual reserved for those who had been "confirmed." Being confirmed is not the same as being baptized. I was baptized but *not* confirmed. Being confirmed was apparently another ritual (probably quite an expensive one) that made one special. I never did understand what being "confirmed" entailed. I assumed one got to wear a frilly new dress, became the center of attention for an entire day, and a booze-up followed by the adults who silently hoped they had successfully mollified God. I never pushed for the "confirmation experience." In fact, there's a distinct possibility that I misunderstood "confirmed" to mean "conformed." It was not a state of being I had any intention of pursuing.

I wasn't allowed to nibble the body of Christ or take a sip of His blood. I was, however, allowed to join the rest of the congregation and wait in line on my knees for the vicar to lay his holy hands on my heathen head. I always enjoyed being blessed by the vicar, whose teeth resembled those of a camel. John was his name, and I felt that he was a good man, albeit a little moralistic, but definitely someone you'd be happy to leave your cat with if you were going abroad for a few months.

John the Camel had an easygoing manner, but when it was time to recite the Creed, business took on very serious overtones. The Nicene Creed was recited from memory by those who failed to realize that we were all being brainwashed. The Creed, you see, was a mantra that reduced the congregation to perform robotic annunciations of a verbal contract that synopsized our required belief. Once the recital of the Creed was underway, everybody seemed to match pace with each other, forcing the delivery to take on a drone-like quality. Another nice, long hymn followed, giving us time to recover from our altered state of consciousness.

I recited the Creed, not realizing that this same proclamation of human inferiority had been recited by similar unsuspecting people since the Dark Ages. I say *unsuspecting* because Christianity was the authority for me and for every other person whose naiveté was hereditary. At age fourteen, I recited the Creed and listened as Christianity's clergy told me how small I was and how mighty God was. No background check was done to prove the veracity of this claim, not by me anyway. Questioning the credibility of the Christian premise never even crossed my mind.

Practicing this weekly routine of praise-offering in the hopes that sucking up to God would win us some sort of favor was a normal occurrence. The Western world seems to call this sucking up "worship." I call it appeasing God's very fragile ego, which we are told is in constant need of stroking. The word *worship* is nice. I like it. I'm sure we'd all like to be worshipped at least once in our lives. But the God of Christianity, being the privileged one, has billions of us doing it *all* the time. Whenever I found myself worshipping God, I always thought, *Lucky sod,* but I didn't question the validity of the act. I just did it because I found myself doing it.

Now, don't get me wrong. I don't think there's anything wrong with a weekly rendezvous in a sixteenth-century church. There's nothing like being a teenage girl with a highly developed imagination heading for a ceremonial evening of remote worship. Walking through a misty graveyard on a freezing winter evening, as the bats that lived in the church's rafters came to life, was always a butt-clenching experience, especially on windy nights. The church warden would battle the weather, and as he wrestled the doors shut, the organ would start grinding. The flickering lights made the altar flowers dance across the shadowy walls, and we stood to attention while the choir sang accompaniment for the vicar as he made his way to the pulpit. John the Camel wore an enormous cross around his neck, so with a prudent "a girl's gotta take care of herself" mentality, I kept a lookout for Christopher Lee. He never did show his face, thank God, and I never did smell garlic.

Once the service was over, we all made a beeline for the pub. The hour-long service had its incentive. We all felt we had pleased God, and for this He rewarded us all with a pint of lager or, for the very wicked, a large gin and tonic. The alcohol laws being a little less radical in merry old England meant a glass of sweet cider was heading my way. Christianity, although a little weird, was fine by me.

Now, some of my readers might propose that so far the only religious practices that I have mentioned that are related to biblical Christianity are reading from the Bible and singing hymns, and that what I experienced consisted of unbiblical rites, ceremonies, and traditions—and Christians, fundamentalists foremost, would be likely to share my distaste. Perhaps this observation is true, but my experiences were and still *are* of the Christian tradition. The cultural practice of worshipping a Christian God happens every Sunday and several times a week across the entire globe—whether the Bible promotes these practices or not.

Anyway, months later, immersed in the culture of Christianity, I partook in further religious customs. During the late summer of 1982, I left Aunty Joan and moved to the large city of Brighton on England's south coast to live with my father, the quite wonderful, warm, and unforgettable Francis Fitzroy Durham. For several months, I had the urge to attend the Sunday service at a large, stuffy church and listen to a load of people speak of godly matters from which I felt extremely removed. These were troubling times for me. I was an out-of-control teenager who felt very insecure due to her life experiences. Don't worry, I was never locked in an attic or made to sweep floors for sixteen hours a day. I just experienced what I now know to be the predictable bullshit that comes from having divorced parents who had no idea what they were doing here either.

I would wake up early on Sunday morning with absolutely no interest in going to church but with a compulsion to do what I thought might please God. Looking back, I don't think I ever blamed God for the difficulties that my parents inflicted on me, but I did think that perhaps God had me under His scrutiny. And from what I picked up from the Christians along the way, I knew He was capable of blessing me or not blessing me. Was I frightened of God? Maybe not. But I was respectfully wary.

Because I had been born into the Christian premise, the perplexing events of my life at that time seemed random and meaningless. I had no idea of the cosmic truth behind what had happened to me, so wariness of God, His motives and also His power, was all that I was left with. Was this fine by me? No, not really.

Children learn by example. The example of my great Western religion, combined with the atheist premise my mother assumed, ensured that I would never, *could* never, find any possible use for it. The useless religion that was bequeathed to me left me with little choice but to assume the same premise that my mother adopted as her own—randomness. Life is because life just is. I believed that life was just one big bundle of chance happening and nothing more.

I failed to consider any sort of spiritual perspective other than the one that turned out to be a sugar-coated joke. I liked the sugar part—all children like sugar—and organized religion was, and still is, well aware of what's needed to entice its potential followers. I was simply the product of my childhood conditioning, and as Friedrich Nietzsche put it, *"The surest way to corrupt a youth is to instruct him to hold in higher esteem those who think alike than those who think differently."*

CHAPTER FIVE

Human Smallness

Historically, the Western God and the stories surrounding Him were the works of an ancient group of influential Semitic males who created a monotheistic religion that is now known to us as Judaism. After the time of Christ, along came a new bunch of men who made some fundamental changes to the Jewish doctrine (original sin and salvation by grace being but a few) and called it Christianity. Later, yet another version of monotheism was produced, Islam, keeping the original phony premise of human smallness intact.

I once asked a Christian friend what she believed the purpose of this life to be. "To serve the Lord," she replied without hesitation.

"To serve the Lord?"

Doesn't this belief *so* make us look like the humans from *The Time Machine?* If we landed on another planet and bumped into an alien race that told us that the premise of its existence was to serve the Lord, we would unanimously agree that it was a subservient slave race submissive to some autocratic master. We'd probably pity them, believing all the time that we were more evolved. We might, under this delusion, quickly find some way of exploiting them. Stooping thus would be an example of our lower impulses manifesting, a consequence of our not understanding our bigness or the God that designed us. On the other hand, some might take a long, hard look at a pitiful species like this and see a reflection of ourselves. Addressing the monotheistic spin on God would happen next, followed by the realization that subservient diminutive beings are *not* who we are.

If I buy a toaster at Walmart, inside the box I'll find instructions written in eight different languages explaining all there is to know about my $12.00 appliance. If I buy Lego bricks, I'll be provided with a beautifully photographed booklet displaying all possible options for what might be built with my new blocks of plastic. I can build a space station or a Formula One race car, and I'm shown, step-by-step, exactly how to do it. If I buy some palm-tree fertilizer, I'll not only be told how to use it, I'll be informed of all the pitfalls of not using it properly. The manufacturers will provide me with a plastic scoop. They will tell me how much, when, and how often to use it. They'll explain all there is to know to ensure that my palm trees have a better-than-average chance of reaching their full potential.

Humanity too is able to reach its full potential, if we knew even a little of the esoteric knowledge that our monotheistic premise of human smallness denies us. How much longer can we recognize as worthy, a religion or *spiritual premise* whose authority goes largely unquestioned in a world of ever increasing turmoil? How can we embrace a religion that gives us only partial truths so that getting through our lives is, at best, tedious and fitful? Knowing the guiding principles for life doesn't mean we'll immediately succeed. It simply means that we stand a much better chance than we once did. Expanding our spiritual worldview means we'll be on the way to reclaiming our bigness—something that holding fast to the doctrines of the Big Three prevents us from discovering.

Now, it might seem to some that I'm being a little over the

top when I relate the damage to our spirituality based on the bogus teachings of the Big Three. But what else can it be when God was sold to the masses as a separate all-creative being and we were told that we amounted to nothing more special than clever, humping, futuristic monkeys—monkeys belonging to a suspect prime creator who prides himself in his role as the Dr. Moreau creator of a lesser species?

It seems to me that the premise of living in a *small* reality created by a separate, all-powerful, all knowing, mighty creator has caused a massive fear-driven consciousness. Is this why, when we look at our history, it seems so bloody and brutal? And why wouldn't it? Believing we are small limits our thinking, and this affects our behavior. To believe that a separate God is ultimately in control of our destiny causes us to feel uneasy. And if we believe our life is not ultimately within our control—we might be tempted to control others. I have done this many times. I believe humanity down the line has in fact been rather busy doing this.

I couldn't understand *why* God created this type of reality, and I couldn't understand *why* humans would particularly benefit from it. For quite some time, I believed that God just watched us suffer so we could humble ourselves and rise up to make better choices reflecting His glory. However, all I walked away with from my bout with Christianity was "Praise the Lord!" The experience left me feeling small, awestruck, and clueless.

Why are we here? For thirty-three years, I didn't have a clue. According to the evangelists who speak on behalf of Christianity, God just wanted us to live here for a while, worshipping and glorifying Him as we went about our business. Hoping to please God by running off to church every five minutes became the Western pastime. We must go to church to receive the good grace of the Holy Spirit and to appease the vague apprehension that any fruit of that grace can be withdrawn at any moment. God, we fear, might revoke His blessings without warning, so we must try to stay on His good side by uttering platitudes like "Blessed be your name!" and "Be blessed through the body of Christ!"

Islam too requires its adherents celebrate their maker's majesty. During Hadj season, those Muslims who can afford it, choose to make an exhausting trip to Mecca. God apparently enjoys watching as millions brave the searing heat to walk around an unimpressive monument in an anti-clockwise direction, a trek that sometimes results in fatal stampedes.

The monotheistic God demands that we pay Him attention. We must worship Him, glorify Him, revere Him, venerate Him, idolize Him, admire Him, bow to Him, love Him, and respect Him. His reputation is as the God of gods, the breath of life, the King of kings, the Alpha and the Omega, the Lord of lords, the spirit of power, the God of grace, Father of Creation, and the Fountain of Life. The Big Three's God also likes to hear that He is the all-consuming fire, the sufficient one, the holy one, the master of the world, the Lord of hosts, the Rock, the source of all truth, the life-giving one, the forgiving one, and the author of life. And as for us pitiable little humans, well, we must continue with our worship and never aspire beyond our lowly position. God likes to be reminded that He is beautiful beyond description, that He is our salvation, the holy and anointed one, the light of the world, Lord of every nation, Lord of the harvest, the name above all names, the restorer of the soul, the star of the morning, the living one, the way, the truth, the life, the purifying flame, the gracious redeemer, the righteous judge, the burden-remover, and the sovereign Lord. He likes to hear all of this at least once a week, and if during the week we feel that

God needs a bit of extra worship, we can always read to Him aloud. Psalm 150 is a good choice.

> Praise the Lord!
> Praise God in his sanctuary;
> Praise him in the firmament of his power;
> Praise him for his mighty acts;
> Praise him according to his greatness!
> Praise him with the sound of the trumpet;
> Praise him with psaltery and harp.
> Praise him with timbrel and dance;
> Praise him with stringed instruments and pipes;
> Praise him upon the crashing cymbals.
> Let everything that has breath praise the Lord!
> Hallelujah!

Or, if we are not quite certain that God has been *fully* reassured of His mightiness, we can always pop in a CD while driving and sing along. From a selection of Christian Reggae, Rock, Country or Gospel, we can serenade God by crooning and chanting songs like: *Savior Lead us Like a Shepard, Nothing Without You, Lost Without My Lord,* or *Wonderful, Merciful Redeemer.*

Actually, according to the tenets of Christianity, humans, by contrast, being small and sinful, are in desperate need of mercy. Mercy has many synonyms—clemency and leniency, among others. We've spent millennia listening to how small and unworthy we are. Then we're told that getting a little pick-me-up from God can help us temporarily rebuild our self-esteem. Praise be to God!

We are, according to Christianity, incapable of doing anything without Him. But the God who made us this way does take pity on us, and from this pity we can receive assurances that it's okay to feel this way. It's okay. We cannot be any different. God understands. God supports us. He really does. God designed us with feelings of inadequacy so His ego could demonstrate its most magnanimous attribute—empathy. God created us with smallness as our main feature But He Himself does not suffer with the same affliction so He is able to help us with ours. Praise be to God!

The Big Three talk of the power of prayer. Except, of course, they are mistakenly praying to a separate God residing in a separate dimension, while we all run around trying to master life without a clue as to who we really are. I have spent endless hours listening to many Christian teachings in the hopes of understanding what it is I am doing here and how I should be doing it. But all I walked away with was that we, being incapable, inept little beings need to:

Pray to the God to whom we have been made to feel inferior.

Implore the God to whom we have been made to feel inferior

Appeal to the God to whom we have been made to feel inferior.

Plead to the God to whom we have been made to feel inferior.

Beseech the God to whom we have been made to feel inferior.

Any feelings of inferiority that might arise in the aftermath must be shaken off so we can sit tight and wait for the Holy Spirit to waft into us, making us better than we were before He arrived.

If we are unable to experience prosperity, we should not whine or fuss. We should be grateful for our lot. And even if we don't feel particularly grateful, there is little point in giving up if God doesn't answer our prayer because we can do nothing without His anointing anyway. According to the Big Three we are small and needy, so we should maintain a stiff upper lip, and when Sunday rolls around, run off to church and drop to our knees; and while we're down there, we can hope that this simple act is enough to satisfy the separate Western God who would be drumming His fingers if we weren't there.

How is it that we've advanced emotionally, intellectually, socially, and scientifically, but spiritually we are still clinging to the same mythology that once belonged to Methuselah's grandparents? The idea that God is the almighty separate One and we are His all-lowly separate creations has caused Western humanity to adopt smallness as the premise of its existence. Our self-esteem has endured this battering for millennia, and it's time it stopped. We must work out the true premise of our existence. Otherwise, the shallow Christian idea that we must pray to a separate God, who is all-powerful and almighty, will ensure we spend quite a bit more time enduring a "little" life— unaware of our human potential.

Here's a thought: Perhaps the monotheistic spin on prayer was strategically implemented by the church long ago because there is a huge amount of money to be gleaned from people who believe God is the Don Corleone of the skies, dispensing favors to all those who pay homage…

"You come to my house on the day of my daughter's wedding, you don't come as a friend, you come asking for favors. I'll do this thing for you. And maybe one day I will come to you."

Puleeeeeease!

(Now as far as prayer goes, I am *all* for it. In fact I think it can determine the magnitude of what one will experience here, but that's for another time.)

Whilst lying in bed, I watched my favorite lady preacher of the monotheistic persuasion speak on matters of human potential, or the lack of it I should say. Joyce Meyer spoke from experience about the modes of behavior she practiced in order to function. As she strode across the stage before the packed arena and told the audience that, if she plucked her eyebrow and couldn't get her tweezers to grip the offending piece of hair, she would implore Christianity's God to step in and put right this appalling situation. I nearly fell off my bed. It seemed that she, while staring at her tweezers, decided that the only way out of the predicament was to subcontract all responsibility for solving her own problems to the superpower in the sky, hoping He would, through her possession of His "Holy Spirit," get rid of her excess facial hair. Principally this means that we humans are to roll over and let 'another entity' take control of all our troubles, problems, quandaries, predicaments, tight spots, dilemmas, setbacks, hitches, glitches, and snags.

I'm sure that when Joyce was recounting this story she meant to invoke humor, but it was quite clear to me that she really believed she could do very little without God's supernatural intervention. The Lord, she truly believed, was the only being in this universe with enough power to be able to tackle *any* problem, from the minute to the monumental. Her unshakable belief was that humans are not designed to take care of anything alone and must turn to the good Lord as our only option.

My children and I recently visited a boarding school for underprivileged, out-of-control teenage boys. The school, the setting, the headmaster, and the agenda were heart-warming ... except for one little problem. When discussing the boys' self-esteem with the headmaster, I was told that the good Lord, being the only one capable, provides for all their wants and needs. The teachers encouraged the kids to implore the God of

Christianity to step in and take care of their problems. Praying for divine intervention was simply taught as the Bible Belt boys' way out of trouble. Eager to carve a better life for themselves, these receptive young "men-in-training" were told that God is the only one who provides. Within the confines of this big God-little human mentality, *self*-esteem was vehemently opposed. These boys are destined to believe that they were designed to experience life as a lowly species—created by a separate God who will gladly judge them as they flounder about in a world of temptation they don't understand.

The above accounts might well represent extreme Christianity, but whether we see Christianity in its most potent form or in a version that is less debilitating, it all boils down to one thing: Human magnitude does not exist. Christianity is the Western world's accepted authority on spiritual reality. From it we formed an idea of who we believed ourselves to be. *Purely* in terms of accomplishment, our current premise of human smallness remains the greatest success the Western world has *ever* seen.

CHAPTER SIX

Heaven, Redemption and Jesus Christ

What *does* it take for the average, garden variety, paltry human to get into the monotheistic Heaven? And what can one expect *if* one should find oneself there?

Many Christians expect death to be *partial* at first. When our body ceases to be, our soul/spirit will find itself in heaven without one. While we are there, some Christians believe that God gives us a temporary body while we wait for our original one to rise up and claim us. The resurrection of our bodies means we will get our original ones back, which might be good news for some but a bummer for others.

"Hi God, Sarah here. I've always believed that when our bodies are buried they rot in a rather timely manner, so if you do intend to resurrect them, can you, *early on*, preserve mine with some sort of shellac? That way, when I get it back, pieces of it won't trail behind me. And one more thing: Because I am not convinced that the blood of another cleanses me of my sins, Christianity tells me that I will *not* get to heaven, but if for some strange reason I do arrive on your doorstep, will I find myself without a body for hundreds of years? Can you tell me how many people have died since the beginning of creation? Are they getting antsy? Are they pissed off that the resurrection of their mortal forms has taken so long? God, can you please do me a big favor? Can you make sure St. Peter maintains an up-to-date inventory of all the people who have died since Adam? This is a big concern of mine. I'm worried that my body might get mixed up with a freaky overweight circus performer with the same name who existed at the turn of the 18th century. Thanks a lot."

"Good morning Sarah, your monotheistic God here. I know you're a little disturbed by the prospect of the resurrection, so being the good Lord that I am, I will put your mind to rest. My dear, the right body at the right time will be brought home, but your soul might find itself there ahead of time. You might have heard it rumored that a body is necessary to experience the fullness of heaven, and without it, heaven's glories are somewhat diluted. Yes, there are some who have found this to be the case, the ungrateful little beggars. A little word of warning might be in order here. Getting a partial afterlife shouldn't wane your enthusiasm, and waiting for your body shouldn't become a preoccupation. The final resurrection hasn't happened yet, and it might not for some time, so don't hold your breath. I know what I'm doing. I've been doing it awhile. Be a good girl, be patient, and remember: I'm watching you."

How *does* one get into the monotheistic heaven? The Catholic vision of the trip presents us with the notion that salvation through repentance is the way out of trouble. And the beauty of this move is that there are no limits to how many times one can repent. You are basically free to sin at noon and repent before your lunch has had a chance to digest. Catholic salvation is nice and easy. *"Forgive me, Father, for I have sinned."*

"Well, say three Hail Marys Vito, and forget about it." You can, in fact, follow this pattern for eighty years or so if you like. Depending on whether a quick trip to the church for repentance had taken place, the Catholic belief is that a verdict, of which God is judge, jury, and executioner, will be issued. One will be sent to heaven, purgatory (an intermediate state for the semi-sinful), or hell.

My husband's great uncle was a Roman Catholic. Salvatore was his name. He was a brilliant man, very accomplished, full of piss and vinegar, with a mass of knowledge and sharp perceptions. Despite all that, he fell prey to the ultimate delusion—that salvation might be purchased. Is this an Italian thing? Or is it a common fancy fostered by all those who are sitting in God's waiting room? Considering the build-up one might have heard about God's monotheistic whims, hedging one's bets would be a wise decision. Sal, faced with ill health and the uncertainty of the timing of his death, decided to go to church faithfully. Moreover, he would write substantial checks to The Blessed Sacrament Church of our Lady, and after a little Sunday-morning repentance, he believed his sins would naturally be forgiven. The Roman Catholic priest became somewhat of a chum, and while failing to address his skewed perceptions, he did oblige Salvatore's wishes by seeing to it that his wallet was a little lighter. Uncle Sal had a reserved parking space on the grounds of the massive church he helped pay for. Being a late riser, he believed that making a valiant effort to get out of bed early and go to Mass, checkbook in hand, would secure his heavenly retirement until he stepped through the pearly gates, which is where I believe clarity grips one with a stupendous revelation. Once through the gates, I am quite sure he would have quickly found himself a secluded spot and a wooden bench. St. Peter, offering him a martini, would have affectionately ruffled his mop of gray hair in an attempt to sooth away his frustrations. But any passerby might have seen him bent forward with his hands on his head and might have heard him mumble to himself, "Goddamn it, Sal, you might have learned to fly by the seat of your pants; you might have learned some of what life was trying to teach you. But overall, you totally missed the point."

I feel bad for Uncle Sal. I am sure when he realized that tithing to the local church did no more to please God than not eating meat on a Friday, he would have said, *"What was I thinking? I could have used that money! Ten percent! I could have bought that Piper Cub. I could have bought that seaplane, and God would have still let me in. What a fucking racket."*

———

Muslims believe in the Day of Judgment. I'm not talking about the final End-Times judgment day, that cosmic joke that unites most monotheistic religions, but a *personal* judgment day. I'm talking about the day shortly after we die in which the Muslims believe one's actions, good and bad, will be tallied. They believe we're being monitored by Allah, who is fair but unbending. We little humans are under observation, in their view of things, and if we're facing some sort of temptation that doesn't fall within the confines of Allah's moral tolerance, we had better take a cold shower and think about the implications of burning for all eternity.

The evidence that is gathered from Allah's unyielding surveillance is not something that can ever be challenged. There's no appeal at this point. What's done is done. Tough shit. Allah gave you one life, and during it you had better get your act together, because redeeming yourself later on ain't gonna happen.

In the Muslim world, redemption can happen only if one has upheld the five pillars of Islam. To go through life strictly adhering to a ridged moral code written by beige males claiming to represent our maker is something that requires a great deal of stamina, to say nothing of self-control.

One is first required to recite the Shahadah: "There is no God but Allah, and Mohammed is His prophet." But what if you had a little too much wine and mistakenly said, "There is no God but Allan"? What happens then? And what happens to poor Allan?

Praying five times a day is another requirement. These prayers include genuflection and prostration in the direction of the holy city of Mecca. But what if you had a really heavy night with Allan, missing the morning prayers because you slept late? What happens then? What if your prayer mat was a few degrees off from the direction of Mecca and you were mistakenly praying towards Macy's? What happens then?

Almsgiving is another prerequisite. But what if, in a fit of selfish fervor, you decided to give only one-thirty-ninth of your income to charitable causes because you had seen a nice little diamanté handbag the week before? What happens then?

Fasting between sunrise and sundown during the entire month of Ramadan is another Allah-pleasing ritual, but what if, under the influence of an uncontrollable urge, you snuck a cookie into the bedroom and found yourself secretly eating it under the covers? What happens then? Can Allah see under the covers?

A pilgrimage to Mecca completes the list of Muslim must-dos. But what if, after spending an entire lifetime saving for this costly trip, a last-minute fancy takes hold Shirley Valentine-style and you find yourself flying off to the Greek Islands for a dalliance with Costas? What happens then?

In his book *Kingdom of the Cults*, Walter Martin nicely sums up the Muslims' perception of their maker: "God is unapproachable by sinful man, and the Muslim's desire is to submit to the point where he can hold back the judging arm of Allah and inherit eternal life in an earthly paradise of gluttony and sexual gratification. Muslims have no concept of God as a loving and compassionate father."

The Muslim version of salvation through "works" (good deeds and moral steadfastness) is something that Judaism also advocates. This implies that God is actually judging us! Salvation cannot possibly come to us through God's judgment because He is not even remotely capable of judgment or, more to the point, practicing *conditional* love.

Now, some of my readers might well ask, "By what method has Sarah Tirri determined which are the true and which are the false attributes of God? How the hell does she know any of this?"

Easy. The premise of this entire book rests on my belief that God does not possess the characteristics, traits, and lower impulses that monotheistic religion has attributed to Him. Judgment? This is ridiculous. Monotheism has created a separate God with a human nature and stellar magic powers who might or might not offer us salvation. This version of our deity not only promotes fear but shortchanges God's omnipotence to the point that many of us simply look at this existence, the world around us and our place therein, with a diminished understanding of the magnitude of what's going on here. We suffer because of this.

Salvation by grace.

"Works" might be what rewards one in the Judaic/Muslim world. Not so in the Christian world. With regards to their depiction behind the process of salvation, "works" is an irrelevant concept because salvation through "grace" happens whether one's works have been good or not. Christian salvation by grace leads to a repugnant non-accountable redemption—but one that will satisfy the lazy.

Christianity's God designed things so that, however we

choose to live our lives, no ramifications exist. All you have to do to avoid recrimination is to accept the idea that someone else died on your behalf in order to absorb (potentially) the sins of the entire human race. It's a one-time deal—just ask for forgiveness real quick in Jesus' name and that'll take care of everything. Don't worry on your deathbed if you happened to have been into child porn, committed grievous bodily harm, raped your sister's best friend, or embezzled your grandparents' life savings. Just apologize and profess your belief in Jesus, for His sacrificial atonement means you too can head straight on up to heaven and be playing eighteen holes with St. Peter the following morning. Instant conversion is the ultimate quick fix. Any and all crimes, including the murder of several family members, the constant beating of your dog, the insensitivity towards your wife's PMS, and failure to unload the dishwasher (when it's your turn) will be removed simply by "believing unto the Lord." The Christian God is the only being that can pardon you as the clock strikes twelve. Last minute, instant absolution simply means saying you're sorry and turning your life over to Jesus. Wipe the sweat off your brow. You're home and dry.

In his book *Elementary Theosophy*, the author and mystic L. W. Rogers writes, "The vital point against this plan of salvation is that it ignores the soul's personal responsibility, and teaches that whatever the offenses against God and man have been, they may be cancelled by the simple process of believing that another suffered and died in order that those sins might be forgiven. It is the pernicious doctrine that wrongdoing by one can be set right by the sacrifice of another. It is simply astounding that such a belief could have survived the middle ages and should continue to find millions who accept it in these days of clearer thinking. The man who is willing to purchase bliss by the agony of another is unfit for heaven and could not recognize it if he was there. Heaven that is populated with those who see in this vicarious atonement the happy arrangement letting them in pleasantly and easily, would not be worth having. It would be a realm of selfishness, and that would be no heaven at all."

On-the-spot exoneration can happen at any time. For some, it conveniently happens when they think they might have glimpsed the end. In the Christian worldview, one can stampede through life, leaving destruction and debris in one's wake, and can then quickly shake it all off a couple of minutes before one strides through the pearly gates of unaccountability. Some, those who are living under the wrong premise, might say, "Why bother converting right now? It takes only a few words and a minute or two. I think I'll indulge my lower impulses and give my ego free rein."

But if these people understood what they were actually doing here on earth and the truth behind the laws that govern their existence, they would know that God is *not* going to be sitting at the other end saying, "Welcome Jimmy. Martha will take your coat. You terrorized your wife, you neglected your children, and you sponged off your mother your entire life. But come in son and sit next to me. None of that matters. There's no such thing as justice in the Christian world. In fact, it's time for you to realize that, for all the good and bad, the achievements and losses that might have resulted from your living, you might just as well never have lived at all. Mary, go and fetch Jimmy a six-pack and an eight-ball. There's a good girl."

The God of Christianity doesn't give a toss about our previous actions. Accepting Jesus so we can join the party is all He requires of us. According to Christianity, we live once, anywhere between stillborn to 100 years, and if during this time we decide the life of Charles Manson is the life for us, God forgives us anyway. If we decide to walk into a school full of kindergartners and kill as many of them as we can, who cares. Jesus died so whatever sins we commit have *already* been forgiven.

Terrorist, Timothy McVey and Mother Teresa are in heaven, right now, hanging out. Mother Teresa resides in heaven in all its glory because she was one of the most self-sacrificing, giving, loving, unselfish women in modern history (I am the other). Timothy resides in heaven in all its glory because he murdered hundreds of people and destroyed their families. The reason the wonderful Timothy is in heaven right now is because, just before he died, he said (allegedly), "God, I am so sorry for this terrible act I have committed, but please, in Jesus' name, forgive me of my sins and welcome me into the kingdom of heaven."

As long as Timothy accepted Jesus as his Lord and Savior, according to Christianity, he would wind up in paradise with Mother Teresa, sipping spring water while enjoying the gentle breeze. Whatever he did before he arrived makes no difference because the slate is wiped clean. In fact, Timothy could have blown up several more buildings and murdered hundreds more children. It wouldn't have mattered in the slightest.

When we consider God bestowing immediate reprieve just by being asked, totally exonerating even Jack the Ripper for all crimes provided he mouthed the right words, we can see that this instant pardon in the Christian vein slows human evolution. If Jack the Ripper had realized, as he walked through the streets of Whitechapel, that he would at a later date choose to feel all the pain of his wrongdoings, maybe he would have thought twice. But Jack the Ripper didn't think twice. He didn't consider the implications of his behavior because the culture that he lived in said that he didn't *need* to. Jack the Ripper murdered and then quickly got his arse saved. According to the proponents of Christianity, he and Florence Nightingale are playing a quiet game of cribbage while enjoying the ambient temperature. And *if* Jack the Ripper had been an atheist, he wouldn't have believed he had a future anyway, so his actions still didn't matter. In fact, the atheist's worldview owes much to mechanistic science, which tells us that, after we die, we will, over a short period of time, become a potent form of human fertilizer. And we can rest assured that, after passing through the digestive tract of the creatures that live in the soil, our consciousness will be quite extinct. This, like the premise provided by Christianity, means that everything we have ever done is and always was entirely irrelevant. Whether one is an unethical immoral atheist, or an unethical immoral Christian, there is no difference. Both have assigned human actions to the dustbin, and what we see going on in the world is largely a reflection of this. According to Judaism, one day after we die, an eternal reward for the morally righteous is on the cards. And if we haven't messed up too badly, according to the Muslims, we'll be rewarded with blessed paradise, or, if we managed to get our arses saved, according to the Christians, we can shake off any implications associated with being a philandering thief and score a place at the right hand of the Lord.

On the one hand, according to the Christians, reaping what you sow is divinely inspired biblical truth, but in the final analysis, Christians also tell us that their God ultimately doesn't require that. Providing we believe in Jesus, we are simply let off the hook without further ado, completely, and utterly, Amen.

Immediate exoneration, from the Christian perspective, might sound wonderful and magnanimous, but if the truth be known, the implications of this instant amnesty can lead one into a false sense of security. Humanity suffers because of this lie, or more accurately, the failure to replace it with the truth. Christianity's portrayal of our eternal destiny superficially depicts God as noble and compassionate, but this portrayal is harmful. How can any doctrine that encourages one to dismiss the cosmic responsibility of one's actions be compassionate? Christianity's account of the destiny of man doesn't encourage one to consider one's actions—you can see this mentality everywhere you look.

Comforted and oh so cozy in the knowledge that the doctrines of Christianity basically turned planet earth into a playground for the unaccountable, Christianity became the prevalent jailhouse religion. The average prison convert (the average child molester, the average rapist, the average murderer) is persuaded by Christianity that he will leave this pointless life and head off for a heavenly round of golf followed by a serene walk through a perfumed garden. Lounging, basking amid the soothing sounds of vestal harp-playing followed by a little nap and an evening in the company of angels is what he is taught to expect for himself.

We will *all* experience the effects of what we have previously sown, this the Bible has right, but we are all destined to become is a lot more special than the role of heavenly tourist. Unlike the small Christian premise that underlies all of Western civilization, no one is coming to save us from an existence of mediocrity and send us straight into another one.

The good Lord provides, as the saying goes, and one of His provisions for the salvation (retirement) of the guilty was His son Jesus. This alleged sacrifice is something that we in America celebrate by collecting pretty painted eggs. Once a year, the anniversary weekend of Jesus' grisly death sends us rushing off to Walmart so we can arrange cheap plastic toys in baskets and tell our kids the Easter Bunny dropped them off on his way through. Is this weird custom perhaps a reflection of our real feelings towards Christianity's weird doctrine?

"And what's weird about it, Mrs. Tirri?" some ardent supporters might still be asking. Well, here's one oddity for starters: Apparently we are going to be saved by the man who failed to save us the last time He was here. Our Savior was previously, and will be again, Jesus. Now, don't get me wrong. Jesus' reputation might very well be deserved. But let's be honest for a moment. His track record is a little iffy. The Savior wandered about, the first Christians wrote His biography, which was widely circulated, and a bloody brutal future was played out by a race that seemingly didn't benefit from His first appearance in any way. Was Christianity's nonsense solely responsible for the troubled future that lay ahead? Well, it seems to me that the fearful notion of human smallness, compounded by the notion that we all need saving, would not have helped us "get it" particularly.

And here we are, 2,000 years down the line, still not getting it and still just as fearful. Is Jesus coming back to this world because He is anxious to set the record straight without blunder or bungle? "Jesus saves" is the mighty message of Christianity. But how do we know He will save? We can't be sure. He didn't manage it before when life was a little simpler. Isn't it time we started working out how we can save ourselves, just in case the modern world proves too much for Him?

The Second Coming.

Some say that Old Testament "prophesy" was incorporated into the New Testament because the early Christians realized that there were limits to how often they could contradict the religion that they were looking to embellish. With a straight face, you cannot take the Old Testament, add to it your New Testament, call it the Holy Bible, and fail to validate what was *originally* written. The New Testament had to give the Old Testament credibility.

The skeptical Richard Shenkman, in his book *Legends, Lies & Cherished Myths of World History*, writes about how certain New Testament stories might have come into being. "It's possible they were added because it makes sense that if Jesus was born in a manger, the manger was in a stable and there were animals present. But historians believe it's more likely that Jesus is featured in a stable with farm animals because the Old Testament says the messiah will be born in a stable with farm animals."

As the King of the Jews prepared for entry into this world, did a star shine brightly to guide those wise men who might otherwise have been uncertain as to where the birth was taking place? Or perhaps the star wasn't a star at all. Perhaps it was actually the headlights of a spaceship belonging to an alien race known as the Ferengie. Perhaps they were hovering about in their spaceships tailing the Magi in the hopes of acquiring their gold, frankincense, and myrrh.

Shenkman says, "Whether they [the three wise men] were guided by a star or not is in dispute. Matthew says they were, but he may have said so because the Old Testament predicted that the arrival of the messiah would be heralded by a star...." Numbers 24:17 says, "I shall see him, but not now: I shall behold him, but not nigh: there shall come a Star out of Jacob...." Shenkman goes on to say, "Where would Matthew have gotten such an idea? It's just a guess, but it may have been from the Old Testament, where he seems to have gotten a lot of his ideas about the messiah. Once again he seemed to be bolstering his case about Jesus by having Jesus fulfill an Old Testament prophecy."

The way I see it, if Christianity was not seeking to align itself with established Jewish scripture, it could have had Jesus born in a cave on the top of a mountain with a stork watching from the sidelines, but Christianity had two choices; they either had to validate the Old Testament or ridicule it.

Like everything else in the Bible, I personally find it all a bit hazy. But Isaiah 1:3 does speak of a donkey and a crib. *If* this portion of Isaiah is prophesy, I am not sure how one goes from "donkey" and "master's crib" to the whole Mary waddles in on a donkey, gets to an inn that is full, continues her labor in a stable, and sticks her newborn in a feeding-trough story. But there you go. Perhaps some ancient scribe leafed through the Old Testament, saw the word *donkey* and thought, *That's it! That's what'll happen. Yes. Donkey. Crib. I feel a plot coming on.*

I can see how building a story around a couple of words might easily happen. Give me the words *butler* and *staircase*, and I could present a grisly story of a pissed-off butler who, one mild April evening, decided to push his demanding paraplegic employer down the staircase in a wheelchair, giving in to a fit of pent-up fury. Or I could present the story of a good-natured butler who spent his entire life traipsing up and down the staircase, patiently and dutifully serving his aging employer, whom he adored and would sorely miss. Just two words give one a great deal of poetic license. My point is this: however you regard it, the Bible is open to much interpretation. And it's the *interpretation* of the monotheistic scriptures turned into "truth" (Judaic, Christian and Muslim) that religious zealots use to rationalize their behavior and terrorize the world.

It seems to me that eradicating sin is a chief requirement of any religion offering us a Savior; but just in case we find a life of virtue too difficult, we are simultaneously offered a Savior who can take a beating on our behalf, freeing us from any implications brought on by wrong action. What a crap job. No wonder Jesus bloody wept!

———

Two thousand years ago, Jesus, a rather hunky hippie (allegedly) came to show us what life was all about. We loved Him. His magical abilities confirmed his reputation of miracle worker. But then, for some strange reason, all that ended. We stood transfixed at Calvary. And as our perplexed mouths remained open, we wondered, we frowned, we scratched our heads, and we thought, *Why, if Jesus could walk on water and wake the dead, could He not just hop off the cross and say, 'Yeah right, Pontius, fuck this shit'?*

The "bravery" of Jesus seems to cause a strange reaction whenever I watch someone who is listening to a preacher speak on the subject. The costly cameras that belong to the multimillion-dollar auditoriums that Christianity currently affords, pan the expectant audience members, whose eyes give away their most secret thoughts.

"Was Jesus brave or stupid?"

God sending His only begotten son into torture is something that I have never been able to get my head around either. Now, maybe my failure to understand stems from the fact that there's something I just don't appreciate about the workings of God, period. Or maybe the torture that Jesus endured on my behalf left me so tainted with guilt that I can no longer think straight. If that's the case, I'm prepared to accept the fact that, shortly after I die, I might. But until then, I'm thankful that Jesus' father was not my father. My father cared for me deeply. I don't think he would have had me stagger under the weight of a thirty-foot wooden cross or let me hang helplessly from nails rammed through the palms of my hands. I don't think he would have stood aside while I was falsely accused, beaten, betrayed, deserted, despised, disfigured, humiliated, mocked, wounded, pierced, scoured, shamed, and left to die in the scorching heat—*especially* if it was to wipe away the bloody sins of a bunch of people who *chose* to behave badly. Sacrifice of the innocent for the sins of the guilty? *What?*

After Jesus ascended into heaven, did He ever stop in His tracks, look around, and think: *What a joke! That was insane. What possible good can come from that little scenario?* Did He then turn on His heels and walk into His Father's throne room, casting a look towards the Old Man that betrayed His unbridled bewilderment? Did Jesus then tentatively stoop before his father and say something like, "Dad, can I have a quick word with you? I'm going to have to be frank. You can't create free will and then get upset when people haven't yet leaned to create well using it. It's just not that reasonable."

The very God that Christianity tells us ordered His son to death is the same God who gave us free will. Why would He have asked another to pay for the implications of humanity handling its free will poorly? Christianity insists that God, the creator of free will, despises the wickedness that our free will creates, and we're all in need of saving! Logic dictates that we must have been designed to experience the outcomes of the not-so-good choices that stem from our free will, because if we didn't experience those outcomes, what would be the point to begin with? What would be the point of exercising our free will without experiencing the delights or havoc of our choices? Why would that make any sense? What could we gain from that? A pointless Christian existence, perhaps.

Jesus dying for my sins is not something that I am prepared to accept as the truth because it doesn't feel like the truth. I was raised with the teaching that Jesus Christ died for the sins of the world; I didn't understand that declaration at the age of ten, and I still don't. Individual accountability for our actions has simply got to be an issue. If you constantly make poor choices and constantly offload the implications of those choices onto someone else, you might feel relieved and free for a time, but after a while, there will come a moment of clarity when you will start to feel lazy and inadequate—to say nothing of what might happen when one approaches the pearly gates.

"Here I am now—entertain me. Oops sorry, didn't see you standing there. Hi God. Nice to meet you. I'm Sid. I died of a methamphetamine overdose. I've been a right bastard. I fathered loads of children I didn't take care of. I lied. I sold drugs to teenagers. I manipulated and left behind mental-graffiti everywhere I went. Anyway, sorry about that. Where's Jesus? Is he busy? Is he chilling? Nice to know he was prepared to take onboard everything I had to give. What a relief that was! I can't wait to meet him. Jesus was the man, the main man, the Lamb of God... What? What do you mean? What do you mean He's not? No! That's not right. What? It can't be. God, that's *so* not right. I didn't know the bloody rules. It's not fair. Where's Jesus? Wah-wah-wah."

While having some foil highlights spliced through my dark roots, I noticed that the salon buzz centered around Mel Gibson's celebrated movie *The Passion of the Christ.* One of the stylists had recently rented it and shared her reaction to it which seemed to have been infectious. Everyone seemed to be in a "wow" state of mind. I was trying to relax and didn't feel like engaging in a religious debate, but I did manage to throw out one question as I flipped through Vogue. After the hairdresser said, "Can you believe He [Jesus] did this for us?" I responded by saying, "Why do you think that He did it?"

The hairstylists all looked as if they were just about to launch into an animated reply, but conversation began to peter out and my question was largely ignored. I sat quietly. I wondered if their initial urge might have delivered the response, *"So we could freely sin without remorse or recrimination."* What other answer could there be? Jesus died on the cross for what purpose? No one in the salon knew, and I still don't.

But of course, it could simply be that Christianity's doctrine of atonement presents us with no mystery at all, and that's because it's bogus. Humankind is not in any jeopardy, and no one is coming to rescue us—and do you know why? Well, I can tell you why. There is no risk to being human! We are not a fallen race in need of saving by some messiah. We don't need one. We just need to understand who we are, not what we have been *told* we are.

Postscript: "Jesus. Listen, sweetie. If for some freaky reason you did actually die for my sins, I would personally like to thank you from the bottom of my heart. If for some reason this is not the truth, then I am quite sure that the preservation of the ancient concept that we all need saving *will* end—but you know this already don't you? Your father is a God of magnitude and He designed an evolving species that *will*, of its own volition, get it."

CHAPTER SEVEN

Hells Bells

What would Hell feel like? Well, I can start off slowly when conceptualizing this, and I will set the scene for you…

Let us consider the case of Rachael, who was 22 when she died, whom God has sent to Hell for not believing Christianity's doctrine of atonement. Rachael's life had always been problematic because her father, an atheist and professor at the University of North Carolina, was emotionally attached to his brilliant career and not to his only daughter, whose neediness irritated him. His detachment marked Rachael. Rachael's mother, an agnostic into physical fitness and her looks, became withdrawn around Rachael's sixth birthday after a cosmetic procedure left her face partially paralyzed. Her detachment also marked Rachael, who did not make friends easily and preferred the company of her pets and her books. Rachel was creative and loved to draw and model clay, but the meaning of life and her place therein wasn't something she gave much thought to.

Rachael died from a virus that attacked her respiratory system. She was not a Christian or a Buddhist or a Hindu. She wasn't anything. She had heard of Jesus, but history, something her father was into, did not interest her and she had never been to church. God's intention was to banish Rachael to Hell, but first, in the spirit of compassion, he thought that introducing her to Hell's eternal misery incrementally was proper and merciful. So God sent her to a soundproofed holding hall, where Rachael and others like her, the unsaved and therefore the condemned, were meticulously prepared for what awaited them for all eternity.

Rachael woke up in her underwear strapped to a gurney in a strange white room with a strange man wearing silvery translucent robes, his eyes ghostlike and indifferent. The man was holding a clothes iron. The stripy cord, which was very long, was plugged into the mains and the iron was set to 500 degrees. The man placed the hot iron firmly on Rachael's belly for three seconds. When he removed the iron, a deep red triangular mark was imprinted on Rachael's torso. Some of her skin had peeled off and was stuck to the iron, but Rachel did not notice the smell of burning flesh because she had passed out from the pain. The man, one of God's angels of a lesser order, injected Rachael with a stimulant and she immediately woke up. The angel had instructions from God to make sure Rachael, and souls like her, only remained unconscious for the briefest amount of time. After all, in Hell, there would be no reprieve from the burning pain. It was better that a soul get used to it. Next, the angel pressed the iron firmly into Rachael's cheek. Again Rachel lost consciousness, but only briefly because again she was revived. Next, the angel pressed the iron into the fleshy part of Rachael's thigh and held it there for five seconds. Rachael screamed and lost consciousness, but again, not for long.

God was looking down at all this from the comfort of his throne room, peaceful and at ease because this transition was merciful. Yes, getting Rachael used to her eternal fate was one of the most merciful acts of his entire lordship.

The following day it was time for Rachael to experience the direct effect of flames. The man had a handheld device with a fuel tank, an oxygen supply, and a trigger. The device was used for soldering metal and reached a temperature of 3,623 degrees F. As she lay strapped to the gurney, the man blasted the flames of the blow torch straight between each of Rachael's toes, holding it there for 10 seconds until the flesh around her nails began melting and bone protruded. Rachel passed out but was revived immediately. There could be no reprieve; a direct edict from the Creator of the Universe. The angel responsible for incrementally and benevolently introducing Rachel to her eventual fate had been doing what he was instructed to do by God Almighty for over 2,000 years. He did not react to Rachael's screams or her pleadings. He had seen it all before. Sometimes he wore headphones and listened to harp music.

The angel used his enormous cache of devices designed to burn with maximum efficiency, and each time Rachael fell unconscious, he revived her with a stimulant. Rachael was tortured daily and systematically in this way for several months, until, on day 97, she lost her sanity. All the while God knew that he was being munificent because getting the unsaved acquainted with their eternal fate was a compassionate act. He had always felt that throwing people straight into the deep end was so unreasonable, and so did St. Peter.

Imagine being in the same room as Rachael along with the silent lifeless angel charged with preparing her for Hell. Imagine sitting on a nice white couch ten feet away for the entire time that Rachael was being partially and systematically burned. Imagine listening to her scream and imagine that no amount of covering your ears would alleviate that sound. Imagine that Rachael was just an innocent kid and the worst thing she had ever done was cheating on her science project by getting her mum to help. Imagine if she was your kid, or your niece, or your daughter…

Have you ever tried to press your hand onto the largest burner on your range and hold it there for two seconds? You wouldn't be able to. Ladies, have you ever burnt the back of your neck on a flat iron? Painful, huh? And it was only against your skin for less than a second. Have you ever walked on black African sand? I have. I had blisters on the soles of my feet for days afterward. Have you ever burned your wrist on steam while removing the lid of a saucepan of boiling eggs? Have you ever removed a roasting pan from the oven using an oven mitt with a hole in it?

I hope you get my point. A god who would torture us for eternity for not believing in a doctrine, no matter how good we have been to others in this life, would not be a god but a monster—and millions have been worshipping this monster for way too long. If you believe that God would torment a person in this way just because they did not believe in a certain doctrine, then you are numb to the highest possible degree, which is the only reasonable outcome when you have blindly believed the egotistical delusions of your pastor or your vicar or your parents.

CHAPTER EIGHT

Eeny, meeny, miny, moe. It's a Random Life, Ho-Ho-Ho!

The Western world largely holds either the monotheistic or the atheistic version of a one-life *random* existence. In other words, it's all just a crapshoot. From all factions of the great monotheistic religions—Judaism, Christianity, and Islam—we observe many adherents making claims about this life and the God who created it. And many a skeptic has thought, *That sounds like bullshit. I don't buy it. I'm outta here. But the skeptical man isn't outta here.* The skeptical Western man unwittingly found himself living under the monotheistic premise that we get one random life, compounded by the lingering worldview of traditional science that tells us the same thing.

The atheist notion of *randomness* diminishes the magnitude of the human experience. For if you believe that you are at the mercy of a random universe, and your life is just an accident, it follows that the idea or concept that you might actually have a specific purpose, is easily dismissed. Also, to believe that hundreds of thousands of people can get swept off the face of the planet, without reason or cause, simply at the whim of an unpredictable natural disaster or airborne virus, then subconsciously the universe in which you are immersed is a dire and foreboding one indeed.

Why does life pan out the way it does? *God knows, but we don't*, is the monotheistic answer. Life just is—the Syrian refugee got his life and I got mine. Who knows why? The child with spina bifida got his life, and Justin Bieber got his. Who knows why? A random life of zero relevance is the essence of the nonsensical (the Syrian boy might say cruel) premise with which Western humanity has been engaged. "Eeny, meeny, miny, mo. Syria's your home—off you go."

It matters not that you experienced one life from one perspective only, or that *what* you did during that life will always remain wholly irrelevant. It matters not that you spent two-thirds of your life on an oil rig. It matters not that you spent a boring eighteen hours a day for forty years down a coal mine (pardon the pun). It doesn't matter that you got only four miserable years under the searing heat of the Ethiopian sunshine. It doesn't matter that you spent your entire life enduring the debilitating effects of rheumatoid arthritis. That was your one random life, the only one that the monotheistic God thought fit to bestow on you. Brad Pitt got a little luckier than you, that's all.

"Hello, Sarah, It's Me again, God. Sarah, my sweet, you are blessed, and those with cerebral palsy are not. Queen Elizabeth II, you are blessed, and those of you living in a Guatemalan ghetto are not. The list goes on. Don't ask why. I don't know why. I felt like it, that's all. *Eeny, meeny, miny, mo—it's a random life, ho-ho-ho!* Listen, shit happens all the time down there, and none of it has any meaning. It has no cause either, not really. The devil likes to mess with you, it seems, but I don't know why and I doubt whether he does either. Perhaps it's just a pissing contest between thee and he."

But if we *are* living in a random world, I would argue that we're actually living in hell. Like me, there are many who have often abhorred their personal situation or the situation of the larger world, and screamed out; *"This is hell. This is fucking hell! Why the fuck is this happening?* "A friend once said to me,

"I couldn't throw myself in front of a bus, but if one came along and ran me over, I'd be grateful." That's a pretty good example of earthly hell, if you ask me. This state of mind happens when one simply believes that shit is happening because shit just happens.

Those of us who suffer this Western affliction (and that's *most* of us) learn to deal with randomness. Being the evolving immortal species that we are, we have no option, really. But know this: Disempowerment of this kind is simply a reflection of the fact that we've failed to comprehend the laws that govern this existence, failed to understand that difficulty, strife, and conflict are predominantly manifestations of us not knowing *how* reality works. Many of us have thought that life is random, a world in which very few experience the magnitude of being human, a world in which very few are aware that our thoughts are creating our own (bubble of) reality.

Although my mother was often swept away by her own brilliance, she always resumed the disposition of a "spiritually unaware" person. My mother was always looking to other people, usually some man, to alleviate her feelings of uncertainty. She was always looking to assuage the (unconscious) nagging feeling that she didn't know *why* her life was happening. My mother spent an entire lifetime looking for "something" but had no idea of the curriculum, so she never knew what that "something" was. My mother's mother bailed out of her life when her daughter was nine years old, and the scars she left behind were never examined by my mother because she believed her childhood drama was accidental and meaningless. She was born into the Western premise that nurtures randomness as the motive behind everything that happened to her. So she never tried to figure out *why* her childhood appeared to have been so brutal, and then it was too late. Her consciousness was that of a severed, often distracted, unpredictably vibrant, permanently mystified woman.

The creation fable depicted in the Book of Genesis spurned a polarity. Another equally dismal account of our existence, is the one being taught in our schools—chance evolution. It's dismal because we're told that it all began randomly. My children are taught that life began with random combinations of gases meeting and changing to create some sort of primeval ooze that *happened* to grow—no design, no blueprint, no intent, and no purpose. It just *happened.*

In *The Stormy Search for the Self,* Stanislav and Christina Grof suggests otherwise: "As modern science discovers the profound interactions between creative intelligence and all levels of reality, this simplistic image of the universe becomes increasingly untenable. The probability that human consciousness and our infinitely complex universe could have come into existence through random interactions of inert matter has aptly been compared to that of a tornado blowing through a junkyard and accidentally assembling a 747 jumbo jet."

Both the evolutionist and the monotheistic offerings regarding the premise of our existence give us no meaning or reason. According to the evolutionists, it was pulled together haphazardly, arbitrarily, casually, and indiscriminately. And according to the Big Three, the law of *cause and effect* is bypassed, totally, and this existence is to be enjoyed and hardship is to be endured. Life on this plane of existence is just a time-filler, really. The Big Three constantly mention the glories of heaven, and this is supposed to help the Syrian refugee get through his ordeal. It is also to help jolly the rest of us along while we're here. Well, as far as I'm concerned, there's a distinct possibility that I will live eighty long years, and just muddling through this life, not knowing why I'm here, is not an option for me. And I don't believe that God expects us to muddle through a random life. Why would God go to the trouble of setting up the whole world just so it could be a place of relative insignificance?

Clinging onto the "heaven-is-the-next-step" fable with detached caution is a popular choice for many. For others, a catatonic belief in the afterlife is common. Either way, assuming that this existence is just a random waiting room for an appointment with the real thing—an afterlife of eternal privilege—encourages many to disregard the magnitude of *this* life.

If a separate all-powerful God exists, why does so much bad happen? If God is the one with the power to put things right, how could He just sit back and watch the ills of the world gather ever-increasing momentum? We've all asked this question.

John S. Niendorff speaks of this God-type in his book *Listen to the Light*. "Are we dealing with an intervening deity who arbitrarily enters the world on occasion for prayer-answering missions, upsetting and defying natural law? Are we thinking of life as an unfoldment of "ordinary" events which, now and then, may be miraculously modulated by our conversations with a Being which steps in and changes things?"

When I was a little girl, once or twice, my secret disdain for the monotheistic God interfered with my unconditional acceptance of Him. My thoughts once switched from praise to blasphemy pretty quickly. *Wow! Isn't God great. An all-powerful God who, with a wave of His magic wand, can change anything? To...,God, I can't believe you're letting my brother get bullied again. They're tormenting him. My mum won't do anything about it. Why can't you make them stop? You can do something, I know you can, but you don't. You're horrible!*

"I am not horrible, young lady. How dare you? I *do* sometimes intervene, but it's my day off today. I don't put-out on Tuesdays. I might be a wonder-worker, but even I need a break now and again...

"Hello everyone, God here. If *any* of you harbor similar thoughts, you'll wish you hadn't. Now, having said that, I'm in a very good mood, and today, I'm feeling rather generous. Today might be a lucky day for some. Yes, yes, I think it will. I have a spring in my step. I whooped St. Peter in a game of golf this morning, and I feel great. It's not often that I get a hole in one. Anyway, let's see, what I can do here?

> Mildred from Bridlington, Yorkshire, your colon cancer is gone.

> Peter from Fenton, Missouri, you are now cured of your impotence and you will win the lottery next weekend. Have fun!

> Ah, yes. Afghanistan. Fatima, I see your husband has been abusing you for years. It's taken me a while to get around to it, but today things are gonna change. The swine you married is going to have a nasty little accident that will ensure that, by the end of the day, he'll lose the use of both arms. He won't be able to beat you with a stick again—unless, of course, he learns to do so with his feet.

> Next, over to Somalia. At two-thirty I'm going to send you a nice little rain storm, so get your

pots and buckets ready and don't say I never do anything for you.

And last but not least, over to the south coast of Spain. Now, don't misunderstand me, I love it when you pray and tell me how wonderful I am. I really do. But Miguel, you're such a baby, stop bloody whining. Your wife's not coming back. She hates you. I know you've been praying faithfully. Thank you for that, but frankly, I'm a bit miracled-out right now."

"Ohhh don't start complaining. I can't help *all* of you! Goodness Me! In any case, you don't live on earth forever. You get to come up here eventually, so knuckle down and take that sulky look off your face. It's not all bad. And besides, Entertainment Earth in twenty-first-century America makes what might otherwise be a dull evening rather exciting. I created the show, and it's a masterpiece of theatre if I do so say myself. St. Peter is really becoming something of a couch potato! Mary pinched his paunch the other day, and he wasn't a happy camper, I can tell you. St. Peter hates to be teased—remember that when you get to the gates. Anyway, we are both rather fond of watching humans who are born into a life that will zap their minds, especially on Saturday evenings, humans who have not grown up with any meaningful spiritual perspective, who believe that life is about sensation, excess, consumption, and intemperance. This is always a healthy addition to any plot. We have tuned in for a very long time now, watching as you grew and grew and grew. You became clever little things, didn't you? And this meant that you now have more hurled at your mind than any species in the history of the planet. You might enjoy some of it, and that's a beautiful thing, but you won't understand much of it. Sensory meltdown is the deal, but all's fair in the field of entertainment. Besides, we do have all of eternity. I'll fill you in on more of the brain-frying plot later. Meanwhile, enough of the West, it's back to channel two. I'm totally absorbed with the action currently happening in the Himalayas. Zeong the hill farmer is helping his wife, who is in the last stages of a very difficult childbirth. She's pissed off because Zeong has got dirty fingernails. Three of their goats have been mysteriously slaughtered by a hairy man with very big feet, and their twelve-year-old boy has just lost his front teeth while wrestling a Yak. Oops! Quick, back to channel four. A global pandemic is about to cause a global recession. Forgive me, but there's so much going on that I get a little beside myself sometimes. I'm going to channel three. The Indonesian air-traffic control tower has lost its power and doesn't have a backup generator. More meaningless random chaos. I love it."

Randomness constricts. This underlying emotion that is now well repressed (and has been for millennia) takes on many guises. Here's an example in which I am speaking on behalf of an authentic but fictional lady…

"My name is Rita and I'm the mother of four teenage boys. I am married to a man who was good enough to rescue me after my ex-husband walked out on us. My husband manages to tolerate my tattooed offspring, who have been indulged with technology and abandoned by a culture that never told them why. My mother-in-law is a cranky old cow, but I will continue to be nice to her because I don't have the balls to be otherwise. My car broke down twice last week, and I know it's just a question of time before it happens again. My husband has promised to take a look but keeps getting side-tracked—the lure of the bar as he travels home at the end of the day offers a little reprieve from the burdens that swamp him. Taking my car to the auto-shop is out of the question because the money my husband earns barely pays our rent, our car payments, our insurance, and the minimum payment on our maxed-out credit cards. I try to pay the other bills from my paltry salary, but when it's time to do the back-to-school shopping, I chew my fingernails while dialing my mother-in-law's number. I like to read romance novels and I like to play the lottery. I daydream of a better life but can't hope to create a better one because I have no idea *how* or *why* this one even happened. Everything just is because everything just is. This makes me unconsciously shift into survival mode. I can't stop evolving, but I'll be doing it mechanically and excruciatingly slowly because the culture I was born into didn't give me any idea of the curriculum. I'll get through my life because I will survive. But I won't particularly expand as a being—because I'm just too busy holding it together."

Expansion is impossible when one is busy constricting. My mother spent fifty years constricting, which was enough for her. She couldn't handle it anymore—she went home. She escaped the planet in a flurry of downshifts, from consciousness to unconsciousness and from life to death. Unlike my mother, some of us who are less afflicted by our random lives might get eighty years or so, but wouldn't it suck to look back after eighty years of life and think, *What the fuck was that all about?*

America's influence over the rest of the world puts us in a strange position. We are an evolved nation technologically speaking, but one that's rotting away spiritually. We in the West are experiencing spiritual genocide because we mistakenly and unwittingly absorbed the monotheistic premise, or said, "Yeah right," and refused to think of an alternative.

Much of humanity has been kept spiritually small by the knowledge with which monotheism supplied it, and to our future's great detriment, when we reproduce, it is likely that our children will adopt the same worldview. We have to expand our minds a little for our children to be able to do the same. Our children will continue a massive evolutionary leap—creating a better world if we acknowledge one vital fact: *Nothing* about this existence is random. Life does *not* just happen.

CHAPTER NINE

The Word

As we comprehend the magnitude of our spiritual reality and explore the truth behind *how* life happens, we should be mindful of *any* religion that insists that it alone has all the answers, because "Being wrong is forgivable—claiming exclusive access to absolute truth is delusional." In fact, we should be wary of any religious order, church, or cult whose proponents purport that they alone speak the word of God, because accepting narrow boundaries of thought can *only* lead to an unawareness of one's true potential and your life might very well suck because of that.

Embedded in the heart of our historical treasure known to the entire world as the Holy Bible are appalling acts of murder, deceit, and religious conflict so intense that I cannot for the life of me assume that its authors were totally above the concept of entertainment. But monotheistic believers who consider the Bible to be the "word" of God Himself will balk at this assertion. Judaism gave us a monotheistic God that Christianity later used to teach the West its spiritual premise. The "word" is the *only* means by which Christianity advocates its authenticity. The "word" is apparently all there is. So, I suppose when one believes with rigid conviction that the Holy Bible is absolute, incontestable, and divinely inspired, any questions regarding its credibility are forever beside the point. Apparently, God suffering from His usual lunacy was something that we simply accepted, overlooked, or, like me, ultimately dismissed. But either way, the Western world still lives the atheist/Christian one-life-could-be-a-bitch premise—gleaned from a religion that offers us all sorts of weird doctrine. In the Old Testament, we can read of a strange fable that tells us of a monotheistic God who created everything and saw that it was good, and when He saw that it was bad, He destroyed it all. Read on. I'm peeling an onion here.

The Garden of Eden.

I've been wondering something. How old did God make Adam—19? 42? Or was it a kind of Tarzan situation whereby he found himself blending in with his environment at an early age, learning to embrace the natural world, making it all part of a wild and rugged maturation experience? Or was Adam an older, more brooding type, who simply sat with his back to a tree, adopting a sulky attitude of dissatisfaction, wishing the bad dream would come to an end? I suppose the appearance of Eve might have helped.

As Adam romped his way across the Garden of Eden in search of a big enough fig leaf to cover his navel, did he ever look down and say, "I wonder what this dangly thing is good for?" After all, he had no parents to point him in the right direction. Adam, we are told, was a brand-new creation. Before his appearance, Genesis 1:2 speaks of a formless desolate world and doesn't speak of the prior existence of life. Now, what we read in Genesis might have satisfied the ancients, who hadn't yet found remnants of one ancient civilization after another, but this can't possibly satisfy modern man, who now has at his disposal some very sophisticated excavating equipment and the ability to be able to carbon date what he digs up.

Editor and author J. M. Roberts, in his book *History of the World,* makes the following statement: "All over the Near East around 5000 b.c. farming villages provided the agricultural surpluses on which civilization could eventually be raised. Some of them have left behind evidence of complex religious practice and elaborate painted pottery, one of the most widespread forms of art in the Neolithic era."

It is now known that brick building in Catal Huyuk, Turkey, was taking place some 6,000 years ago. The Cave of Lascaux, France displays a mural drawn by the hands of men who lived 15,000 years ago. And that's all just recent history. We've dug up a plethora of 40,000 year old skeletons, and in 1974 we dug up Lucy; *she* is estimated to be around three and a half million years old! How credible is the Genesis fable that nothing existed before Adam? Not bloody very, if you ask me.

When was Adam supposed to have been created, anyway? I've consulted many Christians who don't have the foggiest idea. I typed "When was Adam Created?" into my search engine and found a page titled *In the Beginning: Compelling Evidence for Creation and the Flood* by Dr. Walt Brown. He suggests that Adam was created slightly more than 6,000 years ago. Now, this estimate is based on Hebrew texts. Brown speaks of estimates extrapolated from Samaritan and Greek texts that place Adam's creation at 6,200 and 7,300 years ago, respectively. Now, trying to work out when Adam was here sounds like a bore. One might even be compelled to ask, "Who cares?" I know I don't. But the proclamation of the nonexistence of life before Adam's sudden creation comes from a book that we are supposed to believe is the word of God. From this book, the monotheistic premise of reality helped establish our current belief system, a belief system that is depressing and belittling, and this I *do* care about.

Perhaps I'm wrong and Adam *did* suddenly arrive here 6,000 years ago. Perhaps the thriving world that preceded his visit was simply wiped out by God's impatient hand. Perhaps ancient man dealt with many catastrophes that were simply manifestations of God's rage. Perhaps the authors of the Old Testament thought that just mentioning some of God's outbursts was enough to scare us. Perhaps mentioning that the Genesis flood was just *one* in a long line of outbursts from a God who could not control His temper would have been too much for us to take!

Anyway, back to poor old Adam. Could you imagine waking up one morning without *any* memory, only to find yourself in the Garden of Eden? I say no memory because he didn't come from anywhere. He was just plopped down, and *boom*, life was open to his personal interpretation. Finding yourself in the Garden of Eden one morning, having no recollection of *how* you actually got there, *why* you were there, and *what* it is you are supposed to be doing *while* you are there is a bit of a mind-fuck, wouldn't you say? Especially when you hear a strange voice out of nowhere that says, *"You may eat the fruit of any tree in the garden, except the tree that gives knowledge of what is good and what is evil. You must not eat the fruit of that tree; if you do, you will die the same day."* Genesis 2: 16 -17. Did Adam think, Shit, who is this weirdo, and I wonder what tree He's talking about?

I know about trees; I know about fruit; and I know about monotheistic gods—I once was one. I had two Bearded Dragons. They were a dull, but nevertheless pleasing, sort of foot-long reptile that possessed a prehistoric kind of beauty. Tyson and Teresa were their names, and I was their monotheistic god. I didn't ever see them formally worship me, but I did see the look in their eyes that said, "The good Lord provides."

Genesis-style, I provided light, and at 8:00 p.m., I turned off their lamp—providing night. I provided water and separated it from their land. They could see the sky and the moon because their tank sat under the kitchen window. I provided all kinds of plants and fruit as well as living beings like crickets and juicy meal worms. Many might have insisted that the monotheistic God of the Old Testament was as benevolent as I, but wasn't convinced and told them so one night…

"Hi, Bearded Dragons, your monotheistic God, Sarah, here. I will always take care of you. And don't worry, I will never do anything to harm you. Live long and prosper. xxx."

I thought I heard God respond… (or it could have been the Chardonnay)

"Hi, Bearded Dragons, monotheistic God of the Bible here. You Bearded Dragons had better breathe a sigh of relief and be glad that I am not your good Lord. The last time someone took a bite from a piece of fruit that I'd provided, a lot of bad shit started to happen."

⁓⁓⁓

The Christian opinion regarding the origin of man is that God created Adam and Eve and stuck them into the Garden of Eden. Here they had to jump through many hoops and work out what was going on for themselves. Adam and his tempestuous bride, it seems to me, were simply lab rats in God's cosmic experiment—and they failed miserably. God became annoyed that His creation just *didn't get it*. Adam and Eve went forth and multiplied, and when their growing family finally pushed God's patience too far, He, in His apoplectic rage, wiped them out with a massive flood, allowing for new people who were more pleasing.

What was God thinking? What was going through His mind as He planned our genocide? Genesis 6:5 tells us that God was so filled with regret that He said, "I will wipe out these people I have created, and also the animals and the birds, because I am sorry that I made any of them." Was the great magician of the skies composed and calm about it all, or was He foaming at the mouth as he pulled the cosmic trigger?

"God here. Noah, into the ark, son... and as for the rest of you...grow gills or die!"

Was Noah relieved to escape God's vengeance, or did he hide up in the ark in a state of paranoia, wondering if his turn was coming? And what about the other humans who did try hard to please Him? What about Stavros the Greek olive farmer? Stavros loved life, was good to his mother, set right upturned beetles, and worked very hard. Did God deliberately overlook all of Stavros' attributes, knowing full well that he couldn't swim?

Listen, maybe there was a great flood. The planet has been through various cataclysmic eruptions. But are we to believe that God causes them from the safety of heaven, peering down with satisfaction as He watches us suffocate?

It seems to me that biblical conflict, for want of a better term, was not solely a manifestation of man's desire to battle his enemy. Much of the conflict was brought on by God's desire to spar with the little humans that just didn't "get it." Ephesians 5:1 says, "Be ye imitators of God." You gotta be joking! If anyone reading this *does* decide to model the Old Testament God— drowning another in a fit of fury—don't expect to stand in the dock and say, "God got away with it, why can't I?" No one will buy it, not even a liberal California jury.

If I believed there was no spiritual premise other than the monotheistic paradigm, I would definitely want a God who had attributes I could model. But when I read the Ten Commandments, it's clear to me that the God who ordered Moses to tell the rest of the world how to behave had not lived by the same moral code Himself. Thou shalt not murder is a commandment that the God of the Old Testament has broken over and over again. If we are to learn anything at all, shouldn't we introduce the eleventh commandment: "Thou shalt not drown thy creation."

There seems to be many biblical tales that serve as proof that His eminence is in fact not a very nice fellow. Did the idea that God could be so cosmically bored, let alone so cosmically annoyed, inspire the following story?

One day, God decided to *really* fuck with Abraham. He asked him to sacrifice his only son Isaac to prove his devotion. Genesis 22:2 says, "Take your son, your only son, Isaac, whom you love so much, and go to the land of Moriah. There on a mountain that I will show you, offer him as a sacrifice to me." God let Abe take things to the edge, and at the very last minute sent an angel to tell Abraham that the sacrifice had been called off. Abraham had apparently proven his obedience.

Now if that had been me, I would have turned around and said, "You're not God! You're a creep. Asking me to sacrifice my son as a test, or so you can feel better about yourself, is not something that I am prepared to do. Stay away from me and my family, you freak." But Abraham, being a rather amiable Libran type, just grabbed a passing ram—which later became a burnt offering—and carried on his merry way.

The monotheistic God micromanages His human creations and suffers with a similar predicament to that of Joan Crawford when faced with the "hanger problem." Throughout the Bible there are many references to God's quick temper. If His orders weren't met, He inflicted appalling disease. In one instance, nasty boils were to become open sores. "Take that, you bastards" was a dominant sub-theme. God had a nasty little habit of dealing with anyone who failed to conform, and Sodom and Gomorrah would not have been choice places to own real estate. The Bible tells us that God tried it all. He sent plagues of frogs to all those who didn't kowtow, and on another occasion, He decided an infestation of flies would sort them out. And He did this *knowing* that the ancients had no access to a monthly pest-control service.

The Judeo-Christian representation of the workings of God makes it extremely difficult to understand the concept of love. In fact, the God I read about makes Norman Bates appear stable and benign. God was a sociopath of terrifying proportions. Exodus 19:12 confirms this. God through Moses set the tone, and failure to toe the line was met with instant death: "Mark a boundary round the mountain that the people must not cross, and tell them not to go up the mountain or even get near it. If anyone sets foot on it, he is to be put to death; he must either be stoned or shot with arrows, without anyone touching him. This applies to both men and animals; they must be put to death. But when the trumpet is blown, then the people are to go up to the mountain."

Charming.

When we come to terms with the true premise of our existence, we will realize that God actually "created" a bigger reality than we have currently perceived. We will then understand that the Bible might contain *some* spiritual truth—but not the absolute truth. However, if for some fearful reason one is still convinced that the Bible is a total and comprehensive work of divinely inspired truth, then one must also accept the following: God possesses a bipolar mixture of Florence Nightingale-like compassion and Genghis Khan-like brutality—a kind of Vlad-the-Impaler-meets-Mother-Teresa type of deal.

Do many Christians secretly worry whether their God has an anger-management problem? Do they secretly worry about what might take place should *they* become the victim of it? (*Fear*, I think this is called.) Is it fear of retribution that prevents many believers from considering whether it was *man* that actually manufactured this God type? God has been fictionalized, bastardized, and given all the characteristics of an omnipotent but very unwell person. Is the fact that many look around and wonder if this is the best God could do, a reflection of this? I think so.

Various apostles and prophets embarked on numerous attempts to contemplate God and what He required of us. Mohammed, on one particular visit to his favorite hideout, had a vision. This vision (and I'm all for visions) was to become the core of Islam as we know it. But because Mr. Mohammed was illiterate, many other people had the responsibility of recording these revelations. The secondhand nature of creating a truth in this way leaves me a tad skeptical. I don't know why. It's just a feeling I get.

The teachings of Jesus Christ were also recorded by certain men who felt inspired to take on this role. It is now widely purported that, after Jesus' crucifixion, decades floated by before the apostle's rendition of Jesus' life was brought into the public arena. Some say thirty years went by and others say it was nearer eighty, but know this: My memory is vague over last week's events; sometimes I walk into a room and have no idea what I went in there for. Eighty years, huh? No computers, no jump drives, no faxes, no telephones, no tape recorders, no CD-burners, no microfiche, no microfilm, no video recorders, no Dictaphones or whatever else we use to store knowledge,—just 'tablets' and unreliable word-of-mouth communication centering on an alleged event which was, by then, nicely submerged into the recesses of history.

Matthew, Mark, Luke, and John. If I'm going to base the premise of my existence on the ideas of men who needed to rely on the total recall of other men, men who lived in a completely different time, am I not going to run into shades of gray? According to the Christians, I'm not. According to them, the Bible is all I need. Logically, some might remark, "Can't virtually all memoirs, autobiographies, biographies, and reportage as well as all history books be discounted on similar grounds?" And I would answer by saying that very few of these accounts claim to be the undefiled word of God, so the implications that they might well contain only partial truth is not particularly critical. However, the Holy Scriptures are claimed by Christianity to be the word of God, verbatim, and the premise of our Western existence is based on *their* idea of reality. It is critical that their idea of reality be dissected and understood for the fantasy that it is.

Dr. Alan Watts (1915-1973), writer on philosophy and the psychology of religion and consciousness, wrote about the irrationality of claiming God speaks through a single religious doctrine, no matter which religion one might choose, in his publication *The Book: On the Taboo Against Knowing Who You Are:* "...Irrevocable commitment to any religion is not only intellectual suicide; it is positive unfaith because it closes the mind to any new vision of the world. Faith is, above all, openness—an act of trust in the unknown. An ardent Jehovah's Witness once tried to convince me that if there were a God of Love, he would certainly provide mankind with a reliable and infallible textbook for guidance and conduct. I replied that no considerate God would destroy the human mind by making it so rigid and inadaptable as to depend on one book, the Bible, for all the answers."

Internationally revered teacher of world religions, the late Huston Smith, in his book *Why Religion Matters,* mulls the nature of this existence also. With regard to the idea of having everything there is to be known about existence revealed in a single book, he draws on the sentiment of Søren Kierkegaard when he says, "Although we *think* we would like to be told, if we *were* told we would not like the position that would place us in. For it would deprive us of our freedom and thereby our dignity, leaving us robots. All that would remain for us to do would be to look up the answers to our questions in life's answer-book and apply them mechanically to our problems."

Nightmare, sweetie.

The answer to the question "Should we believe that scripture, as it survived our barbaric past and completed its passage into the modern world, is without any element of manmade distortion?" is a resounding *yes* for all Christians. Yes we should.

The following Baptist standpoint, taken from the official website of the Southern Baptist Convention, reaches levels of dogmatism that leaves me speechless (well, not quite.): "The Baptist Faith and Message: The Holy Bible was written by men divinely inspired and is God's revelation of Himself to man. It is a *perfect* treasure of divine instruction. It has God for its author, salvation for its end, and truth, without any mixture of error, for its matter. Therefore, all Scripture is totally true and trustworthy. It reveals the principles by which God judges us, and therefore is, and will remain to the end of the world, the true center of Christian union, and the supreme standard by which all human conduct, creeds, and religious opinions should be tried. All Scripture is a testimony to Christ, who is Himself the focus of divine revelation."

How do we know that the Bible is a "perfect treasure" and not a mixture of some truth sprinkled throughout with some error—embedded in what could be termed a literary magnum opus? How do we know that all scripture is "totally true and trustworthy" and that God is judging any of us? Isn't the above unreasonable? Irrational?

Each monotheistic religion expresses its message of faith, each offering a variation on a common theme, and within each religion, each sect offers up its own version as divine truth. The Baptists give us their special spin too. According to the Baptists, all scripture is a testimony to Christ, who is Himself the focus of divine revelation. I believe He is *perhaps* the focus of divine revelation, but I don't believe *all* scripture is a testimony to Christ. This leads me to the next point. How do we know whether the appearance of the Christ figure and the events surrounding His physical appearance were actually historical events? I don't know whether these were true events or not. Like much of what came before, we can only speculate as to the truth of the matter let alone the details. But one thing's for sure: Christ is embedded in the consciousness of Western man. Whether He was physically real or of mythological origin is not, I believe, of any great significance. *His* story has shaped humanity's experience of itself; the "Christ consciousness" is what's real and bona fide. *Believing* there was an actual Christ figure amounts to the same as *knowing* there was a Christ figure, except, of course, when you're dealing with the Christian belief that "Jesus the man" will physically come back to this earth to save those who believe in Him and leave behind those who don't. This is where a *significant* parting of the ways happens.

"Jesus the man" is *not* coming back, but perhaps His consciousness is, because His role, like any other great avatar to have walked this earth, was to offer us an example of what it means to *get it*. Whether a man or a myth of the era, Jesus was ahead of His time, expressing ideas and perceptions that shot beyond biblical consciousness into the future—serving as an invitation powerful enough to spur future change. Perhaps we are all destined to be the embodiment of Christ. Perhaps an 'awakening of consciousness' is upon those ready for it. Perhaps we have indeed reached an end time. And if this is so, it might be more progressive to assume that it has nothing to do with the fearful end time crap that speaks of a helpless humanity in dire and desperate need of rescue. There's only one thing we need rescuing from, and that's the monotheistic religions that misunderstand the breadth and scope of Jesus' mission, entirely.

Chinese Whispers.

Now just for argument's sake, supposing St. Paul, among others, *did* channel God's very word. How do we know that this original truth, as it made its way through the ages, remained just that?

If I tell my husband something I deem to be true, and he tells his sister, who then tells my father-in-law, I can tell *you* from experience that the original truth will now have added dimension to it. If my father-in-law then tells his other son, who then tells his wife, the original truth has now turned into a partial truth. Partial truths are not *necessarily* partial because they were partial truths to begin with. They might have become partial because the information changed hands many times before it reached its final destination. To arrive at a partial truth doesn't mean that the assertion in question was fraudulent in its entirety; nor does it mean that something was truthful in its entirety. It can simply mean that either something was omitted or something was embellished.

Translation.

Material is translated from one language into a second language so that the readers of that second language don't have to know the *first*. That is the purpose of translation. It is therefore not necessary for the layman to be familiar with the mood and culture of the ancients. It is not necessary for the layman to acquire a deep insight into the mythology of the Semitic people or to gain a comprehension of Greek and Hebrew syntax. Grounding in the nuances of all the Mediterranean languages with weird alphabets—not forgetting the ancient ones like Latin, Coptic, and Aramaic—is not something he need bother with either. We don't need to study the origin of words, their earliest etymological root and subsequent forms; we can happily rely on the precision of history's biblical translators.

The written word of God came to us through the hard work and (hopefully) the diligence of the men commissioned to *translate* the bible, and afterwards, the men commissioned to *reproduce* it. We must trust that, as they fulfilled their scholarly obligations by comparing and revisiting the original tongues, they managed to encapsulate the sentiment of the Bible's authors with integrity and honesty.

Before the invention of the printing press in the sixteenth century, Bibles had to be handwritten by a scribe. So, imagine it is the year 1152 in a little village outside Canterbury, England, and Thomas à Becket's third cousin twice removed, John

Barnabas, rubs his hands together and pulls his robes around his aching shoulders. Contemplating the enormity of his task, the scribe peers at the Greek text to be translated and begins the painstakingly slow method of its reproduction. Hoping to produce the Book of Genesis in time for spring, the process of dunking his quill into an inkpot, blotting the excess, checking to make sure he hadn't skipped a line, fills the scribe's winter months.

This was how the early Bibles (for hundreds of years) were put together. A fair question might then be: Due to exhaustion, absent-mindedness, inattentiveness, ineptitude, incompetence, or profound backache, were any of the biblical scribes responsible for omitting, embellishing, losing, removing, altering, or distorting scripture as it was copied by candlelight? Did they drink alcohol while working? I know I have consumed a fair bit of wine while writing this book. One time I started seeing double and thought I had saved a file when in fact I had deleted it. What if the scribe in question possessed a burning creativity that was constantly rearing to express itself? What if, when translating Deuteronomy 8:2, the scribe decided the story would be much more dramatic if he changed the amount of time the Israelites spent in the wilderness from 4 years to 40? What if he read the Greek texts and thought, *That's not what needs to be said—God damn Greeks, I could do a much better job.* What if the scribe was a budding Tarrantino type, and just for shits and grins took the words "love disobedient children" and translated them into "stone disobedient children"? Deuteronomy 21:18-21. Who would have known?

Is it logical to look for complete and absolute truth in any religious teaching? Is it logical to look for total truth in ancient texts, which have been reproduced by the billions? In this book, I use references from an assortment of Bibles. I decided not to standardize my quotes using just one version of a King James Bible. Instead, I used the Bibles that have somehow found their way onto my bookshelves. I have a Good News Bible that my Aunty Joan gave to me. This particular translation seeks to state clearly and accurately the meaning of the original texts in words and syntactical forms that are widely accepted by people who use the English language as a primary means of communication. I have a huge gold-leafed leather-bound Roman Catholic Bible that belonged to my husband's uncle. I love it; it smells musty and holy. I have another called The Journey. I bought this when my children were babies—when I was still loyal to the idea that Christianity spoke the truth about God. I have another, left by the Gideons (whoever they are), which I stole from a hotel room in Hong Kong during my days as an Air Stewardess. (I don't know how it happened. I found it along with the hotel hairdryer in my suitcase when I arrived back in London.) Another dog-eared version of the Bible, with the strange picture of *Christ Glorified in the Court of Heaven* by Fra Angelico (National Gallery, London) depicted in flame-red on the cover, sits next to another which has very thin pages. This latter Bible has a poignant inscription from a mother to her university-bound son, and dotted throughout are colorful pictures of religious happenings (Moses and the Burning Bush, etc.) And I have one with a bright white pseudo-leather cover that I bought for a steal in the dollar store. Actually, I bought four of these, one in green, one in baby blue, and the other in navy. I have no idea why.

In all, there are twenty-six versions of the Bible, and all have been translated into an incredible number of different languages. These Bibles have all survived the reign of our wonderfully friendly, peace-loving ancestors: the Romans, the Vikings, the Anglo-Saxons, the Greeks, the Turks, the Huns, the Mongols, the Moors, and recently under the watchful eyes of various (or is the word *dubious?*) popes.

When you look at the hand-me-down nature that got the scriptures to where they are today, should we not assume that, even though our scriptures might represent God's word, they actually might also represent some of man's? To maintain that divinely-inspired scripture has not been meddled with during the course of our barbaric past is not helpful. To deny the fact that man has even been barbaric, selfish, ruthless, greedy, power-hungry, and malevolent, harboring very different agendas unrelated to the quest of enlightening the masses, is less so.

As I turn the pages of the Bible, I do see partial beauty and perhaps partial truth, but I also see a lot of stuff that leaves me thinking, *You gotta be fucking joking—God inspired this nonsense?*

While looking around at the world, cringing at the human condition, one might theorize that there's something we're not getting. It is now the duty of the Western world to discern between truth and manmade distortion. Misunderstanding God and the reality that He created means we misunderstand ourselves. This is not good. This is why many of us feel a nagging dissatisfaction and then kid ourselves that we don't. Most of us have no idea what we are doing here, and we have no idea why we are doing it. We must question the premise of this earthly existence and know that, as Thomas Huxley stated, "Every great advance in natural knowledge has involved the absolute rejection of authority." We must reject the authority of the monotheistic worldview. (Absolutely.) We must form a new spiritual paradigm by updating and expanding our beliefs about who and what God is. Anyway, what's wrong with updating the opinions of the ancients? We've redrafted, updated, and revised the Constitution of the United States of America on the grounds that part of what it said no longer served us. The Constitution as of 2021 is only 234 years old.

Once our views have been updated and revised, our redraft certainly won't attribute such catchy sayings to God as "if a man lies with a male as with a woman, both of them shall be put to death" (Leviticus 20:13) or "I will strew your flesh upon the mountains, and fill the valleys with your carcass. I will drench the land even to the mountains with your flowing blood" (Ezekiel 32:5-6). The reason we won't attribute God as saying these sorts of things is because the religions that created a false God will be examined and their second rate theology *dismissed.*

We *can* establish truth in this end time. We can absorb what we consider to be the truth, the whole truth, and nothing but the truth. We can do this because we are an evolved Western nation. We live in the 21st century, and we can think for ourselves. We'll be the judge of what makes sense and what doesn't, and in doing so, we can open our Bible from time to time because "We can do all things through Christ which strengtheneth us" (Gospel according to Saint Paul). We can sift through the bullshit and find the truth (Gospel according to Sarah Tirri).

CHAPTER TEN

...and man created God

Who is responsible for the way in which the Western world currently views God and the reality He created? The answer: Christianity of Roman lineage.

The masses, the ordinary, the common folk, people like you and me, satisfied the early parts of our evolution by living in clans and remaining mostly ignorant of all but those areas of expertise required to survive. Securing food, shelter, and defense was our common concern. Most people couldn't read and were led by the Church anywhere that institution cared to lead them. So, in a nutshell, a separate monotheistic God permeated human ideas of *reality* at a time when we, the masses, were illiterate and the early church fathers were able to influence what was fed to us. We were preoccupied with staying alive, not with accumulating, let alone questioning, knowledge. We had little choice but to defer all thinking to the intelligentsia, who also advised the court. And if you found yourself in the uncertain position of advising the white male who got to make the decisions, you did so in a "yes sir–no sir" manner. Aided by their advisers, a plethora of power-hungry men have molded humanity's experience throughout history. King Henry VIII is a perfect example of someone who was freely able to shape the experience of our ancestors who lived at the mercy of his whims. (And he is recent history.)

Henry VIII was in the position to influence the law and beliefs of the land. And influence those laws and beliefs he did. The state-issued religion of the day, Roman Catholicism, said that divorce was not permissible. Henry, being Henry-the-King-of-bloody-England, didn't have to stand for that. He needed a divorce, damn it, and a divorce he would get. If the Pope wouldn't comply with the king's wishes, then the king would divorce England from the authority of Rome. The Vatican's power over England would become nonexistent, and Henry would do as he liked. The Church of England was born and Henry's marriage to Katherine was annulled. Henry then rubbed his palms together in anticipation of a new babe. Except, of course, Henry soon became tired of that one too. No problem. The Tower of London was right around the corner.

Was this man just messing with everyone? No. He simply maintained his existence by exerting supreme control, that's all. If his intentions were questioned in any way, he simply chopped off the head of the questioner. Henry might or might not have felt the need to justify his actions, but if he did feel the need, he could have done so with perfect ease and mass acceptance from his subjects.

Henry VIII, an egotistical maniac who reigned during a time when his behavior would go unchecked, could have done *anything*. Did he wish to influence his subjects by instilling in them his view of reality? Was the realm of religion of any particular philosophic interest to him? Did he attempt to use religion to keep order or scare the masses? Did he even *care* about the masses? Who knows? But it is my guess that he could have done whatever he wished. My point is this: the further back in history we go, the easier it was for a ruler to exert supreme control.

Since time immemorial, many "great" men have been in complete control of their lives—and everyone else's—and made any and all decisions freely and with perfect ease and the further back we go, the more power they likely had and the less chance they had of that power being questioned.

For me, the *Anno Domini* Romans are prime suspects. I've seen *Gladiator*, I know what went on. As far as I'm concerned, any of those twitchy tyrants of Roman blood are chief candidates for insisting that their religious worldview become the staple of the Western mind. Creating *any* spiritual premise would have been a piece of cake, and selling it to the masses by claiming that their priesthood represented God would have been easier still. Implementing *any* doctrine was just a question of rounding up the scriptures, commissioning the work of a few chosen intellectuals bankrolled by the state, and boom, "reality" is born (or reborn).

Constantine the Great.

As I sought out ideas that would satisfy my questions regarding God and the nature of the reality He created, I often came across negative references to Constantine the Great. He was allegedly the one who established the very religion that "his lot" once tried to stamp out. His vision of a cross in the sky was followed by a vision of Jesus. Now, don't get me wrong, I love visions. I have a few myself. But when one's visions contribute mightily to Western humanity's idea of itself, they can be a real bummer. Following his vision, Constantine unashamedly went about the business of spreading the doctrine of human smallness across the entire Western world. It's a doctrine that still shapes the premise of the world in which we live.

The means by which the newly-converted Constantine managed to convince Rome that Christianity was *the* thing has come under a great deal of scrutiny. Many have said that he slaughtered his way to power and then embarked on a zealous "convert or die" campaign. This kind of ultimatum typified the way things got done in that era, but it was an affliction not confined to the ancient world. A thousand years later, we are told, Pope Gregory IX instituted the Inquisition. In the interests of keeping "social order," the inquisitors did not wait for complaints but sought out and dealt with anyone whose beliefs were not aligned with the papacy's. (I would have been so screwed.) "Do or die" was a choice to which the masses were forced to submit—there was no third option. And our submissiveness further strengthened the religions that required it. Powerful men, of which there was a diverse supply without a break throughout the ages, roamed and ruled, bending God's creation to their debauched rendition of the divine plan and insisting we do the same. The Romans were hedonistic bad asses. They might have been responsible for a lot of cool infrastructure that helped humanity's evolution (plumbing remains my favorite of their inventions), but they were also responsible for massive crimes against the very people on whom they were trying to impose civilization.

Did ancient governing mean managing the masses from a framework of corruption and self-indulgence mixed with select unelected, one-sided, undemocratic power—all sealed with a bribe and a handshake? Influential, adept men converged to form an "all-new" religion that set the tone for the premise that the modern West endures. The collaboration ensured that the participants walked away with feathered nests—outlandish material rewards, titles, and privilege. And the future race (us) were left with a legacy of monotheistic nonsense, a premise that is *not* serving an advanced culture.

Anyway, back to Constantine. Who knows what ran through his mind. Maybe he had an over-inflated ego. Maybe he had a huge sexual appetite that was never satisfied, leaving him to seek out a bit of warfare and violence as a means of sublimation. Maybe he wasn't as bad as many think. Maybe he genuinely believed in the goodness of his actions. Maybe he had a big heart and his inclination for religious fervor has been grossly misreported, and maybe, just *maybe*, he had no concept that the premise of human smallness that he fought to make mainstream would make its way successfully to a future 1,700 years away.

Whether or not Constantine did convert a vision into "proof" of Christian truth, is of little importance to me. I really don't care. But I do care that the premise the Romans ultimately promoted still gives us the idea that we are humans of sublime mediocrity submerged in a reality consisting solely of good versus evil created by the hand of a separate (monotheistic) God who Himself does not experience the crap that we do.

Has God ever looked upon the Western world and taken to His bed with shame and grief? Has He ever been seen, by a privileged few, gazing at the ceiling fan while wondering when we're all going to get it?

"Hello, God here. You must stop listening to those monotheistic men who speak on matters of which they have no idea—Jew, Muslim and Christian. There are a lot of them. Please try to understand that life will only become what you want it to be when you realize the magnitude of who you are and what it is that I actually did. Countless men who have claimed to serve me by proxy throughout the ages have actually served themselves, and the premise of your existence got rooted in their illusions. Apart from the later addition of Islam, the Jewish-Christian alliance is the Monotheistic monopoly that you endure today, and after all these years, you still have no idea what you are doing here let alone why you are doing it."

CHAPTER ELEVEN

Revamp it!

Did you know that the tenets of Christianity are simply an assorted blend of previous religious practices? Until recently, I didn't.

Now, as a means of "producing" a religion, I don't think it's a bad one. I am a fan of the idea of bringing together a diverse mix of metaphysical and philosophic thought, and therefore, I don't actually have a bone to pick with Christianity regarding the *means* by which it came into being—my contention lies in the monotheistic message of human smallness it delivers.

Now, one might ask, "By what method are we to determine that Sarah Tirri is speaking the truth whereas the white males of the past were delusional liars who distorted humanity's relationship to God?" Well here's the method: The only way one can determine whether I, and people like me who hold similar views, are speaking the truth is to ask, *Is this the best God could do?* Wait for the answers. Answers will come. And one will quickly see that those who terrorize the world are faithful to the monotheistic worldview, and that it's the monotheistic ideology of big God-little human that has caused more trouble for humanity than any other. Look at the evening news, where you will find that this is still the case. One might then ponder whether monotheistic religions brought forth their delusions and lies because they saw that distorting humanity's relationship to God was profitable. Not only did they glimpse the rewards attached to keeping humanity "small," but seemingly, they had access to a lot of previous mythology that could be redrafted and revamped to support their purposes.

Many scholars have been busy concerning themselves with the authenticity of the Western world's monotheistic God and how He came into being. In her book *The Christ Conspiracy: The Greatest Story Ever Sold,* Acharya S. says, "Christianity's history is rife with forgery and fraud. So rampant is this treachery and chicanery that any serious researcher must immediately begin to wonder about the story itself. In truth, the Christian tale has always been as difficult to swallow as the myths and fables of other cultures; yet countless people have been able to overlook the rational mind and to willingly believe it, even though they may equally as easily dismiss the nearly identical stories of these other cultures."

As a result of some rather sober scrutiny, many now concur that the creators of our monotheistic religions simply mimicked the ideas of the ancients, reestablishing them in new bangles and bows. It is widely purported that Christianity and Islam simply revived and remodeled the religions of antiquity; there is nothing original about any of it except its packaging. Despite their different observances, Christianity and Islam have suspiciously similar stories, dramas, superstitions and events that came from the ancient cultures of the B.C. era. The Sumerians, the Semitic people—the Babylonians, the Phoenicians, the Assyrians, the ancient Egyptians, and the Hebrews—established and treasured a fine cache of religious ideas, enabling many to later find inspiration from their collected stories. The Aztecs, the Mayans, the Incans, and the many aboriginal cultures offered us ideas to forage too. We know that the adept ancient man was skilled in the art of astrology, and from those who worshipped the sun gods, we inherited a legacy of first-class ritual, ceremony, sacrament, custom, and rites.

In his book *The Secret Teachings of all Ages*, Manly P. Hall writes about the originality of Christian philosophy and the suppression of alternative spiritual ideas: "The early Christians used every means possible to conceal the pagan origin of their symbols, doctrines, and rituals. They either destroyed the sacred books of other peoples among whom they settled, or made them inaccessible to students of comparative philosophy, apparently believing that in this way they could stamp out all record of the pre-Christian origin of their doctrines. In some cases the writings of various ancient authors were tampered with, passages of a compromising nature being removed or foreign material interpolated."

Jesus' birthday is celebrated on December 25th, but is there *evidence* that he was born then? December 25 is also the date that the Roman pagans celebrated the birth of the Persian sun God, Mithra. So one might conclude that you are in fact getting gifts because some deity named Mithra was said to have been born on this date.—Merry Mithramas!

Manly P. Hall says, "Saviors unnumbered have died for the sins of man and by the hands of man, and through their deaths have interceded in heaven for the souls of their executioners. The martyrdom of the *God-man* and the redemption of the world through His blood has been an essential tenet of many great religions.... The list of the deathless mortals who *suffered* for man that he might receive the boon of eternal life is an imposing one. Among those connected historically or allegorically with a crucifixion are Prometheus, Adonis, Apollo, Atys, Bacchus, Buddha, Horus, Indra, Ixion, Mithras, Osiris, Pythagoras, Quetzalcoatl, Semiramis, and Jupiter."

The idea that humanity is in need of saving by the blood of another is central to Christian doctrine. Nothing's new. Apparently the spin-doctors of greater antiquity presented us with their fall guy and told us the same thing. Indeed, various male heroes of the ancient world, whose role it was to save humanity, can be linked to Jesus' role, and the link between Krishna's mission and that of Jesus has not gone unnoticed. Krishna, the charismatic Hindu Savior, apparently came into the world, like Jesus, to help rid the world of vice and establish virtue. It didn't work though, did it?

Reciting the parallels between the mythological heroes of the ancient world and Jesus would take too long and, besides, there are *so* many people who have already done this. But anyone wanting to broaden his knowledge of Christianity's conception should enter "Savior cults of antiquity" into his search engine and take a deep breath.

Now, it's possible that the "Savior message" was a comfort to us at some point during our evolution, but isn't it time to understand that the *small* premise we in the Western world are living under is still partially based on the *small* premise given to us by an ancient religion that includes mythological stories of very ancient religions. The act of embellishing a former religion and naming it something new is not a problem for me in itself, but the idea of repackaging an ancient religion as a means of continuing to shortchange God and the reality He created has to stop. The premise of our existence, as hauled throughout the ages, remains small and it needs updating. We are not an ancient race—we are an advanced race. The "masses" now have access to cardiac surgeons, gynecologists, neurologists, optometrists, chiropractors, and podiatrists. A thirty-week-old Western fetus stands an excellent chance of thriving. We help the handicapped; we help the elderly and the hard done by. We educate our children; we understand their psychology to a much larger degree than ever before in human history, and the Department of Children and Families intervenes if their parents fail to do their job properly. We don't scorn lepers, jeer at gladiators, or crucify people with different beliefs (I hope). There are many among us who would gladly adopt a Romanian toddler with AIDS. And seeing as we are no longer terrified of contracting someone's mystery disease, palliative care of the terminally sick is considered normal. In many, many ways we are becoming more humane and more compassionate. We are in fact evolving. Our children are offered scholarships to first-class universities and are given opportunities that once were available only to a select few. Any man from proletarian origins, given a few votes, can rule the world. We have built the Hoover Dam. We manufacture satellites and low-carb energy bars. We do a lot of things fantastically well, so, you might well ask, in these times of comparative lucidity and progress, how has modern man *not* managed to rid himself of ancient concepts that no longer effectively serve an advanced race? What's taken us so long? Perhaps G. K. Chesterton's observation might help: "Tradition means giving votes to the most obscure of all classes, our ancestors! It is the democracy of the dead." We *have* honored our ancestors and we have served their legacy. It's time to serve ourselves. It's time for us to understand what *they* didn't.

CHAPTER TWELVE

Morality, Sin and the Catholic Church

Many Christians revel in the idea of Christ's return to Earth, and for many, the sooner the better. As Christ ushers all the believers to His Father's house, most will consider this an infinite improvement on this war-weary and sin-cursed world that many of us currently endure. Well, I too am pretty weary of our war-torn world, but when looking to improve it, could we please discard such superstitious ideas that sin is the result of a curse. A curse! Adlai Stevenson. said. "For my part I believe in the forgiveness of sin and the redemption of ignorance." Me too.

The Christian worldview is that some of our choices can result in offences, misdeeds, felonies, minor to major faults, misdemeanors, transgressions—in short sin. I believe our life here is more an issue of trial and error—in short a divinely-designed *evolution*, at least after some point of mechanistic adjustment to the environment. We learn from our experiences and grow accordingly, we evolve.

As we encounter life and engage with it, we should freely respond to our evolution in a manner which bespeaks profundity of vision. Guiltless and hopeful, we can be sure to find ourselves saying things like ... Yes! That worked. That worked really well. That was a good idea. We can improve on that. That was a failure. Fuck that. We must learn from that. Well, we'll know what *not* to do next time! That was a big success. That will *not* bring us what we hope for. That caused a lot of problems. That's not going to cut it. Fantastic! We handled that like a bunch of amateurs. Damn that was good! That wasn't. Our finest hour. We took a long time to recover from that. We made the right choice that time. That was brutal. We want more of that. We need less of that. *Oh no not that.* That was great. No it wasn't. Trial and error.

Christianity not only rejects the human experience as one of trial and error—the Christians label the human experience sin and assert that we were each *born* into it! To be born is to inherit the title of sinner and deal with the natural feelings of inadequacy that a chip on the shoulder like this creates. Well not me sweetie. You can count me out. Listen, I might have been born into a lot of things, but sin wasn't one of them. I was an innocent, pure, evolving, divine little being from the get-go, and I still am. However, I am sure that any good Christian pastor would quickly tell me that I have ideas above my station and urge me to recite the Sinner's Prayer, which goes something like this: "Father, I come before you humbly to ask that your Son Jesus Christ would take away my sin. I believe that you sent Him to earth and He died here on the cross and that He rose from the dead three days later. I believe that by the shedding of His blood I will have eternal life. I accept Jesus as my personal Savior from this point on, and thank you for sending Him to atone for my sin. In the name of the Redeemer Christ Jesus, Amen."

My God, if I get to heaven and meet a fat Christian preacher from San Antonio, Texas who says to me, *Sarah, I sinned. Jesus paid the price—so let's have a party,* I think I'll slap him.

Saul Bellow said, "A great deal of intelligence can be invested in ignorance when the need for illusion is deep." I don't believe in the concept of sin. It's an illusion of smallness. But if I did believe in the concept, I would rather atone for my own sins, thank you very much. Having them atoned by the blood of another might do nothing more that promote me to the grueling realms of heavenly selfishness that Christianity tells me *is* the blessed afterlife.

Sin. Sin. What is sin exactly? If sin is acting in a way that does not get divine approval, then I have "sinned" many times and I doubt whether that will end. I have had sex out of wedlock. I love wine and may very well get deliciously drunk on my next birthday. I have yelled at my kids, and although I am successfully working on this, I may very well yell at them in the future. I have tried to love my neighbor as myself, but there have been times when I have thought *if he turns up the volume one more time I'll let his fucking tires down.* I have broken the speed limit: When I was nineteen I drove away from the scene of an accident (no one was injured) to avoid getting breathalyzed. The law quickly caught up with me and I had eleven points issued to my driving license, but because the female judge empathized with the fact that I had no choice but to drive to work, she didn't revoke my license. I have had an abortion, which was the worst moment of my life. I have, on several occasions, chosen not to submit to my husband but told him to go fuck himself instead. I use bad language from time to time. I think Howard Stern is funny. I have masturbated. I do accept God as the ultimate morality and meaning of life, but I often forget to pray to Him and find myself reading a Kingsolver novel instead. I try to beware of idolatry, I really do, but sometimes God seems to take a backseat and instead I focus on personal ambition, sensation, and accumulating possessions. I try to remember the Sabbath, but just a few weeks ago I had some friends over for dinner and we forgot to meditate on obligations, family, prayer, decency, kindness and justice; instead we swam in the pool, downed some beer, and watched Robin Williams perform a hilarious stand-up. I have tried to honor my father and mother; but they'd let me down so many times that, although I did manage to honor them most of time, there were times that I just didn't have it in me. I have never cheated on my husband, but if my husband ever committed adultery, I might succumb to my lower impulses and be tempted to follow suit—just to get back at him. I have stolen: When I was nine years old, I stole a chocolate bar by setting up the perfect decoy to distract the shopkeeper. I have cursed the lawn service for mowing when it was too wet to do so. Have I ever borne false witness? Yes I have. I covered up for my friends many times who were accused of smoking in the school toilet. I covered up for my son once too. Doing so contributed to the maintenance of harmony in my household—I don't regret this decision. I have coveted my neighbor's possessions; some time ago my neighbor planted some breathtaking palm trees, and for a long time afterwards, I wished they were mine. Do I sin? Yes I do. I sin all the time.

What is my biggest sin right now, at this very moment? Some Christian apologists might assert that writing this book and challenging Christianity is a sin, perhaps a mortal one. Leslie Stevenson, in his book *Seven Theories of Human Nature,* talks of the reaction that I might get for doing so. "Christianity is a closed system: …the believer can take the offensive against criticism, by attacking the motivations of the critic. The Christian can say that those who persist in raising intellectual objections to Christianity are being blinded by sin, that it is their own pride and unwillingness to receive the grace of God that prevents them from seeing the light."

A good way to nullify a debate before it begins! I think I'll try it myself.

The Big Three's monotheistic premise of human smallness has left some with the erroneous belief that a separate God knows best, and *what* He knows may or may not be revealed to us. Furthermore, some believe with conviction that God is actually testing us. My housekeeper believes that the reason she is forever up against tedium and lack is because God is not happy with her. As she puts it, she has not been going to church and tithing and therefore not doing God's Will. He is forever making her life difficult as a way of suggesting to her that she really should get back on track.

Just recently I watched a show on the A&E channel that focused on the intriguing topic of Faith Healing. The interviewer was talking to a Latin couple who had recently been to one of Benny Hinn's crusades. As tears rolled down his face, the man spoke of Benny Hinn's inability to heal his son's brain tumor and believed that God *took* his son because he had sinned in the past and this was God's way of punishing him.

How many people out there believe that God is capable of punishment? How many people out there believe that negativity happens because they have disobeyed God's Will?

German philosopher Friedrich Nietzsche was skeptical of the belief that God *has* expectations and man lives to do His will. He said the following: "What is the meaning of a 'moral order of the world'? That there is a thing called the will of God which, once and for all time, determines what man ought to do and what he ought not to do; that the worth of a people, or of an individual thereof, is to be measured by the extent to which they or he obey this will of God; that the destinies of a people or of an individual are *controlled* by this will of God, which rewards or punishes according to the degree of obedience manifested."

Codes of conduct are set by all those who believe that God requires obedience, but let me tell you something about God: God requires that we evolve in a world of experience—examining what we find out about ourselves and understanding that we create our own reality as the result. Nothing more. God doesn't approve of a middle class, dutiful, tee-totaling churchgoer who finds anal sex and homosexuality repugnant any more or less than he approves of an overly-made-up barmaid with breast implants and two children fathered by different men. He feels for us—but He is not judging us.

As Erich Fromm said, "There is perhaps no phenomenon which contains so much destructive feeling as moral indignation, which permits envy or hate to be acted out under the guise of virtue."

I once had an abortion, a grisly affair, and for many years afterwards believed that God viewed me as an unrighteous slut—lacking in moral fortitude. (I felt this once, I don't know.) If I'd have felt that I could have carried my baby to term and parted with it, I would have done so. If I'd have thought that I could have mothered my baby single-handedly and given it the best, I would have kept it. I did neither—I had an abortion. God doesn't look upon me any differently than someone else who might have chosen differently in a similar situation. I don't regret having an abortion, but I *do* regret getting pregnant in the first place. Upon reflection, I learned a lot about myself during what was one of the worst periods of my life. Carelessly getting pregnant so I could experience one-upmanship over a married boyfriend who I couldn't really stand was a learning curve that forever revealed to me aspects of myself that definitely needed work. One way or the other, I will evolve. I will evolve as I experience the reality that I create for myself. I will learn to create from a bedrock of integrity, honesty and truth—not from seeking external power by attempting to exploit those with whom I have formed manipulative relationships.

The narrow parameters of acceptable experience that the Big Three advocate *will* suffocate us. Many are gasping for air already. God has expectations and rules from above—the essence of the Monotheistic worldview. We live below, and the best we should aspire for is to lead a morally pious life hoping this premise fulfills our experience here. Sanctimonious moralistic scrutiny is epidemic in the Western world, an attribute of smallness that contributes little to the positive progression of human evolution. This is what we see all around us: people hurting, suppressing their evolution towards self-realization, lying to themselves because guilt (from inside) and condemnation (from outside) attack them otherwise. To act in a way that we have been taught is not acceptable to God makes us wary, isolated, secretive and lonely, and people living in restriction of this kind will have a harder time relaxing and realizing their divinity than ever before. Praise the Lord.

As Joseph Collins says, "By starving emotions we become humorless, rigid and stereotyped; by repressing them we become literal, reformatory and holier-than-thou; encouraged, they perfume life; discouraged, they poison it."

The moral fundamentalists would like homosexuals to believe that we will all benefit from such individuals suppressing their sexual-inclinations in order to uphold man-appointed standards. I beg to differ. I think it would be in the best interests of every homosexual across the land to embrace anything that would otherwise prevent him or her from knowing and experiencing *who he or she is*. Biological errors or birth defects don't exist in the real world. God is in control of everything He created.

If we have an inner, very present, never-ceasing tap on the shoulder, it should not be ignored in favor of some virtuous moral standard that has nothing to do with virtue and absolutely nothing to do with morality. The natural divine flow of life might be experienced by more if we chose not to repress what is naturally very real. Repression undermines God's design and will do nothing more than cause a frustrating dormancy of inert feeling—a counter-evolutionary measure that a backward worldview encourages.

Now, here it's possible that some of my readers might be inclined to ask, "If an inner tap on the shoulder is not towards homosexuality but towards various other behaviors—bestiality, necrophilia, and incest for example—are those feelings also to be explored? If not, why not?" Here's why: If one wants to have "unlawful" sex with a sheep, better make sure the sheep in question is a willing participant and is licking his lips in anticipation of the experience you have planned. If he runs away, or the only way you can shag him is at the edge of a cliff, this is clearly a violation. In short, only willing participants in any act make it an okay act. Force anything on another, and yes, you are sinning.

With regards to necrophilia, I suppose the act depends on whether one has prior permission. For the record, my husband does not have my permission to fuck me when I'm dead. And if he proceeds to do so, a violation of my will is indeed taking place.

With regards to incest, I have yet to hear or read of any cases in which one person involved was not controlling the other, either physically or psychologically or both. If addressing the inner tap on the shoulder of which I speak means that someone else will suffer as a result, the inner tap on the shoulder should be *reclassified* and the root of it explored—*not* acted on. Pray to the higher power—get help—stay away from people until you do. I watched my mother succumb to the influence of one particular husband quite often. Her husband, my stepfather Roy, was always trying to control and diminish others in an attempt to bolster his ego and temporarily blot out his own feelings of self-disgust. Look around you'll see people like Roy everywhere. My mother was perfect for someone like Roy, she was looking to come under another's control. In a warped sort of way, this made her feel safe. She fell at the feet of such men and became submissive to them if she thought they might love her. One day, she decided to rid herself of her children in an attempt to please her husband who despised them. Roy controlled her. She would have done *anything* for Roy.

What we choose to explore and how we choose to do it should *not* interfere with the well-being of those with whom we share the planet *in any way*. We share this planet for the purpose of growth. The narrow-minded people who run around telling us that growth born of a world of diverse experience is not righteous might find themselves in need of a lot more experience to rid themselves of the emotions to which narrow-mindedness gives birth. The fundamental moralist who spent his entire life judging and condemning the behavior of others is going to be in for a hell of a shock when the pearly gates swing open. This same fundamentalist is going to be in for a bigger shock when he plans his next life as a drag queen hoping for a sex-change operation and a life in the Las Vegas spotlight. Narrow-minded bigotry might mean that some spend hundreds of karmic years living out the physical expression of their prejudices—an easy thing to let happen when you've neglected compassion and totally misunderstood God and the reasons He created this world of multiplicity.

Honoring one's true feelings is not an option for those who believe that endurance is a prerequisite to pleasing God. Hold your head up and forge on, or keep it down and pretend this sanctimonious act of suppression makes the world better. Such self-torture won't make the world better, of course. How can it when suppression induces exactly the opposite of what God intended.

Whether one believes that life is an endurance test or not depends on whether one is able to see the bigger picture or the smaller Christian one; my angel, Aunty Joan, saw only the Christian picture.

I am still sitting on the fence about this, but I have often felt that the experiences that my Aunty Joan believed she must endure, and the amount of self-discipline that she practiced in order to maintain her charade of a marriage takes my breath away to this day. She stayed married for more than fifty years (until her death) to someone she might have been better off divorcing forty years before she left the planet. Uncle Jim, her nearly loyal, long-suffering husband, endured a sham of a marriage too, because guilt would have plagued him otherwise. Guilt-free, Uncle Jim should have held his wife's shoulders and said, "Duck, in a strange way I do love, but I can't take this anymore. I will provide for you, I will be a father to our children, and I will be there if you ever need me, but our marriage is driving us both insane." Mentally, he probably *did* say this as he reached for his valium, but nothing ever changed except the dosage and his level of resignation.

By most onlookers, Uncle Jim was pretty much regarded as the persecutor and Aunty Joan the victim. Their interaction, if you can call it that, was subdued with contention. Aunty Joan, for better or worse, decided to ignore the fact that her husband completely ignored *her*. She busied herself making sure the church magazine was delivered on time. Aunty Joan pruned the roses ready for the new blooms to grace the altar at St. Mary's, and her declaration of denial meant that Uncle Jim would remain lost and all alone, frustrated and bemused.

Celebrating the realization that they had made it through another intolerable day, Uncle Jim and Aunty Joan would climb the stairs and fall into separate beds, knowing that all they had in common was a marriage without passion. Masking the fact that they were fundamentally incompatible, Aunty Joan would insist that his *mental health* was to blame for their torment. "He's a very sick man, dear," she would say while tying her apron. I realized years later that perhaps he wasn't sick—perhaps he was *desperate.*

I sided with Aunty Joan. The fact that Uncle Jim wouldn't respond to her would provoke me to say things such as, "Throw something at him! Make him say thank you when you hand him his favorite home-baked apple pie with extra dollops of clotted cream."

But Aunty Joan would smile and say, "Sarah, duck, he needs my compassion. He's a very sick man."

Looking back, I would say he wasn't in need of her compassion. He was in need of a reaction. He never got a *reaction*, though. I think it got buried under the Bible.

Divorce would have liberated them both, but it was out of the Christian question. Aunty Joan would continue to read the Psalms as she acted out her marriage with ferocious fortitude. The stigma of divorce would have been too much for her to bear. Proud of her peaches, Aunty Joan continued to bake Uncle Jim's favorite dessert, and he continued to reach for his pills. And as for me, I watched the most fucked-up marriage I have ever seen play out.

Now, some readers might say, "What about this marriage,

as you describe it, is Christian? Biblical Christianity teaches that husbands and wives are to be 'one flesh' and are to love one another 'as Christ loved the church.' Your Aunty Joan's marriage was not built upon Christian precepts because she didn't fulfill the edicts of the Holy Bible's dos and don'ts."

I would answer this by saying that my Aunty Joan was the epitome of someone who believed she lived a Christian life. She might not have fulfilled *all* aspects of what it meant to be a Christian wife, but she was doing the best she could within the parameters of the Christian doctrine that demands that a wife submit to her man.

⁕

The Roman Catholic Church.

The throne of St. Peter is the grand old seat that currently belongs to the man who was elected to become what some might call the modern-day Jesus. He didn't just arrive; he was voted in. And he quickly picked up the reins of his all-new divinity. Marvelous. The Pope will travel around in his amour-plated Cadillac, waving his hand through the air, wafting grace at all the people who believe he speaks of the way, the truth, and the life. His mission apparently is to proclaim the gospel of Jesus Christ—whatever that means, but I don't think it means upholding an antiquated institution by suppressing God's true spiritual premise and replacing it with one of monotheistic smallness.

The Roman Catholic Church and I have different perspectives on many religious issues. Pre-marital sexual abstinence is one of them.

A friend of mine had a daughter who decided to practice the Christian art of abstention. She married the son of a Christian preacher who too was waiting for a marriage certificate before copulating. They dropped thirty grand on their church wedding and divorced five months later. Superficially they appeared to be well suited, but whatever went on under the bedcovers ensured that a Decree Nisi would ultimately be the only thing they had in common.

Had I followed the tenets of Christianity, I too would have been forbidden to have sex before marriage. But I *did* decide to have sex before marriage, and I am glad I did. Otherwise, I would probably have quite a few divorces racked up by now.

According to my husband, sex is the greatest thrill known to man, but the Pope simply believes that God created us to partake in the sex act for the purposes of procreation and the proper expression of conjugal love *only*. If this is the truth, sex is off-limits to much of the population. If I believed the Roman Catholic God was real and created our sexual urges to fulfill this limited expectation, I would be inclined to believe we are the products of some botched experiment that God and His entourage during our 'creation stage' are responsible for getting wrong.

"Hello, God here. If any of you ever have sex outside of marriage, know that I will utterly disapprove, and you don't want my disapproval, believe you Me. Disapproval might mean my compassion on Judgment Day wanes. Oh please, don't start whining—just take a cold shower. I had no idea I had left your creation in the hands of such incompetents. I was only gone for twenty minutes, and when I returned, your instinctive desire to copulate went through the bloody roof. There wasn't a damn thing I could do about it either. Alarm bells were ringing, warning lights were flashing, but no one seemed to take any notice. You just can't get good staff these days. Anyway, what's done is done. I still require that you be married to have sex. I am not going to change my entire plan just because some fool didn't do his job properly."

In his book *Breaking Faith: the Pope, the People, and the Fate of Catholicism,* journalist and author John Cornwell writes affectionately of the priesthood. "Most of us treasure these men who hallow our marriages, usher our children into the life of grace, console us in bereavement. Priests seldom become close friends to the laity, but they are the embodiment of Christ's intimacy in our lives. The special place of priesthood in Catholic consciousness only serves to make their current tribulations all the more tragic."

What are their current tribulations? Backed-up testosterone levels, I suspect. Or else the suppression of their desires has greater blowback than many of us care to imagine. How else can we explain the sordid perversions of some of the Catholic laity?

Robed men in positions of power control other men by telling them that they have to abstain from sex forever and ever Amen and live in this manner to please God. But I doubt whether God is very pleased, and I'd bet He's far from impressed. And just in case one is still apt to ask, "How is it that Sarah Tirri has come to determine who is the *real* and *right* God?" I would answer by saying that I believe in a God who shares and welcomes our happiness wherever it is we can find it. I don't believe in a God who approves of our misery, *especially* if it is disguised as chastity justified as a form of spiritual fitness. Hope and faith in a *God of Magnificence* is the method by which I attempt to establish the *right* and *real* God. Every time. And if there are any potential priests out there who feel the need to turn their lives over to God's work, make sure you've got the right God. The real God doesn't get a kick out of watching any of us attempt the torturous process of suppressing what it means to be human. The monotheistic God might, though.

"Hello, monotheistic God here. I hereby formally address my potential clergy: All of you who are contemplating life in the priesthood, listen out for your calling but know what you're up against. Unless you walk a fine line and agree to absolute chastity, temptation might send you to places you'd be better off not visiting. If you fail to exert supreme levels of self-control, you will likely experience huge amounts of anguish, and some of you might well find it wholly unbearable. But it's just a little spiritual endurance test that won't last forever, so lighten up. You'll be here soon—unless of course you mess up, in which case you won't be. Ouch! Also, I have seen some of you look at me and shake your fists. I have seen that sorry-assed look throughout the ages. But, predictably, you quickly realize the futility of such outbursts and pray like mad that I'll forgive you. This does indeed warm my heart. I'm a monotheistic God, demanding yet merciful. Oh, and by the way, a little tip from one who loves you: Try using your left hand—it might feel like someone else. Oops, I forbid masturbation. Sorry. Even I forget the rules and regulations occasionally. Arrivederci."

You might be asking yourself, "Do the pious demands of Roman Catholic restriction portray God in this sick light?" I believe so. I believe God is peering at the pontiff as I speak, wondering how this lunacy gained mass acceptance.

The overt amount of sexual posturing that we in the West are now seeing (I've watched a Snoop Dogg video, and I know what goes on) is just a reaction. Any belief that a strict adherence to a decree that wages war with our instincts means a backlash is *always* inevitable.

Now, one could twist this line of reasoning to also mean that the insistence upon strict adherence to laws against murder and theft result in *more* murder and *more* theft. I would suggest that most of us are not repressing a desire to murder *or* steal, and the fact that murder and theft is forbidden by law doesn't present us with any particular temptation to break that law because these are not acts resulting from our instincts. Those who kill and steal do so because they feel powerless. I don't believe they *instinctively* enjoy killing someone and stealing their wallet afterwards.

The pendulum *will* swing and we *will* find a balance. We might very well have to go full circle before that happens, and that's okay, because we have all the time in the world. We might have to watch as clitoris-piercing becomes the new girl-about-town expression of sexual liberation (God forbid), but whatever form it takes, you can bet your arse that exploring our sexuality is what's on the agenda for a humanity that has so far been encouraged not to do this.

CHAPTER THIRTEEN

Fanaticism of Islam

The early inhabitants of Arabia may very well have experienced an evolution of culture and learning, but now it appears that evolution has stalled in that part of the world and things are getting out of hand—and the rest of the world is far from impressed. This, I suspect, has something to do with the Muslim's rigid monotheistic premise—a premise of human smallness that has bred fear into the most susceptible, the bloody results of which are now on display for all to see.

Who are most susceptible? All those who found themselves believing in a separate God, an all-powerful Allah who went to all the trouble of creating this magnificent diverse reality for the *sole* purpose of having *all* of us righteous little humans bow before Him in reverence and fear. For this Allah rewards us with a blessed afterlife which Muslims refer to as paradise—a paradise no less, which is expected to be the embodiment of the material world that we infidels are condemned for embracing.

In his book *Islam Revealed*, Dr. Anis A. Shorrosh writes, "Pious believers in Allah can expect abundant sensual pleasures in paradise. There will be perpetual luxury, physical comfort, food, clear water, mansions, servants, lovely maidens and virgins." With the exception of the virgins, my husband and many men like him have all of that right here. Look at Jay-Z or P. Diddy. What's the big deal?

In his book *Children of Allah*, Folco Quilici writes, "Man is always attracted by a love of desirable things: women, children, heaped up stocks of silver and gold, thoroughbred horses, flocks, and cultivated lands. All these are accessories of earthly life but he (*the Muslim*) must forget them all and turn toward God."

Many Muslims renounce (and despise) the material world in favor of a world of asceticism, but to my way of thinking, much of what the Western world enjoys now is the great expectation of the Muslim's view of the afterlife. If Mustafa Hussein Abdul Rafsanjani leads a life of virtue, Allah will supply him with all that the Western world enjoys in the here and now. It seems the average Islamic youth desires the Western experience but feels that God requires him to die or martyr himself before he can experience it.

The thought of spending eternity in heaven receiving *more* instant gratification in the company of Allah bothers me—but I don't suppose that I should worry too much. Like the Christian God, I don't think Allah has me on his guest list. But from time to time I have been known to uphold a couple of the five pillars of Islam, and so just in case, here's a thought: What if, as I step into paradise, I find myself thinking, *This is familiar; I had similar birds and trees in my backyard?* What if I get to my future mansion and think, *Um, it's not much bigger than the one I just left?* What if I had already experienced cultivated lands and a healthy helping of gold and silver? What if I look at my new servants who are staring at me wide-eyed and expectant, and find myself immediately thinking, *Oh no, not again, another looong training period.* What if monotheistic heaven is just a cosmic extension of the materialism that the Western world created and nothing more?

If it is, I ain't going. Well, maybe I will for a *while*. Maybe curiosity would get the better of me and a trip around cosmic hedonism would be fun. But for how long—a month, two months, two years, ten years, 100 years, maybe 500 years? The band members of Mötley Crüe could probably handle thousands, but as for eternity, *nah!* I don't think eternal excess would work for me. I'd burn out. I'd get bored. I'm easily stifled. I'd get antsy.

To score a place in paradise, one must live a life of sobriety, temperance, piety, abstinence, and self-denial. Allah's clergy tell us that absolute compliance to the tenets of Islam will shape human conduct in a manner that gets divine approval. This might be okay for the self-disciplined, but as for us inquisitive types who frequently slip into bouts of self-indulgence and excess, well, Allah's not going to tolerate it. What happens when the average Muslim wakes up one morning and realizes that his conduct the night before has seriously ruffled his maker's feathers? One can always repent, I suppose. Remorse might help. A lot of time spent in prayer might reveal Allah's merciful side. Then again, it might not. One can never be too sure with a monotheistic God.

If I were a Muslim and believed in the validity of Allah, I would be shit-scared of Him, that's for sure. I would suppress any instincts I had to explore life's fullness and hope that eighty years of chastity and devout subservience pleased Him sufficiently that He might greet me down the line with a conciliatory smile and say…

"Al Salaam-a'alaykum, Sarah. Well done. Your self-discipline and sacrifice prove that I am the ultimate maker. You didn't dare not toe the party-line did you? I needed to scare you into obedience, you see. I needed your assurance that I was the almighty, and this was a perfect way to do it. I have always kind of known it really, but you know how it is, it's nice to have a billion or so people perpetually knee-jerk before you. Everyone needs a little pick me-up, and I, Allah, have needs too. Come on in, Sarah, and look around you. You're in paradise now, so relax. That hellish little planet that you just left represents nothing more than a test of your deference for me. Me! Me! Me! Anyway, there are a lot more people left to kiss my arse where you came from. I don't need you anymore. Your eighty-year-old wrinkly body has served me well. Despite a few hiccups, which I magnanimously overlooked, you venerated me pretty consistently, and for that I reward you with a blessed afterlife. I am a merciful God, really, I think. What do you think, Sarah? Do you think I am merciful?"

"I'd be pretty stupid not to agree. Oops, shit, I hope you didn't hear that. Sorry, let me kiss your ring. Yes, Allah, I think you are very merciful. Allah o Akbar!"

The prophet Mohammed, it seems, experienced his share of divine fear. Islam informs us that, while Mohammed was in a cave, the Angel Gabriel paid him a visit. Geoffrey Parrinder, in his book *World Religions: Ancient History to the Present*, tells us, "According to the traditional account Mohammed was alone in meditation when an angelic being commanded him to 'recite' in the name of God. When Mohammed failed to respond, the angel seized him by the throat and shook him as he repeated the command. Again Mohammed failed to react, so the angel proceeded to choke him until Mohammed was finally compelled to do as he was told. Thus began the series of revelatory experiences that were the chief mark of his prophethood and whose record constitutes the chief work of Muslim scripture, the Koran."

Because of our misplaced desire to be tolerant of the tenets of all religions, *human weapons* are produced right under our noses. The Middle East, and the Muslim communities established on foreign soil, shelter those who are building and those who become, weapons of mass destruction. Terrorists. But psychologically, *what* causes a normal, healthy baby to end up as a human weapon? Well, I can tell you. Fearful, cradle-to-the-grave indoctrination of *the* most debilitating kind—preached by *the* most powerless-producing, God-fearing monotheistic faction of them all. Islam.

Terrorists were not terrorists at birth. They were innocent, cooing little bubbas just like any other baby. Their fearful religion, forced onto them by ignorant, fearful fathers, fucked them up. There's a tongue twister: *Freaky Fanatics From Fearful Fucked-Up Fathers.*

Countries like Afghanistan provide training camps where the *last* stages of preparation, the fine-tuning, take place. Recruiting a potential martyr can be possible only when the potential martyr is not very well to begin with. I know that if you asked the average Western youth whether he fancied a trip to an Afghan training camp followed by a suicide mission, most would look at you like you'd totally lost the plot. I'm quite sure most well-adjusted Muslim youths would too. You don't live a life of relative normalcy and then at age eighteen hop out of bed one morning and think, *I know! I'll strap a load of Semtex to my arse and blow up some infidels!* The sort of depravity that births a terrorist starts very early on. If my newborn son hadn't been handed to me but into the custody of some Islamic extremist instead, it is likely he would have turned out a very unwell person.

The mindset of the extremist will be bred into their children. No shouts of encouragement from an enthusiastic cheerleading

Mummy. No jumping into Daddy's strong arms who then becomes the Pillow-headed Ninja Master. No pillow fights. No *Green Eggs and Ham.* No Happy Meals with extra honey-mustard. No Chuck E. Cheese's. No proud winks. No kissing the boo-boo and putting endless Rug Rat Band-Aids on it. No movies. No huge buckets of popcorn. No gold stars. No comfort blanket. No sleeping in Mummy and Daddy's bed when you are pretending to be ill. No sleeping in Mummy and Daddy's bed when you are *genuinely* ill. No Santa Claus. No field trips to the Science Center. No running around the neighborhood on Halloween, pretending to be Spiderman. No food fights. No "Come on, darling, I know you can do it. See? I knew you could, you clever little thing." No Kodak moments. No unstoppable giggles. No comfort. No pets. No friends. Just the Koran—handed to you by a parent who fears this existence in the same way that you one day will.

In a much less radical form, I once came across a little boy who was quite clearly a product of his conditioning. I was helping my sons' second grade teacher teach cursive handwriting, and a new boy appeared in class, mid-term. Andrew had been raised in cyberspace. He lived a very different reality to that of my sons, and the school considered him a special case. Once I "reached" him, he animatedly spoke to me of his missions to steal disks, retrieve top-secret information, and scale walls; he talked of bad guys, laser beams, and secret codes. This "reality" overshadowed the external world he will be required to participate in, and his manner was distant and somewhat shifty. His communication and writing skills were poor, his attention span even poorer, and his future, uncertain. But one thing is certain: He is only reacting to the stimulation provided to him by his environment. If he had been removed from his birth situation and placed in different circumstances, he would be a completely different boy. God bless him.

Anne Bancroft, in her book *Women in Search of the Sacred*, featured the stories of some noteworthy women. One, Jung Chang, grew up during China's Cultural Revolution and speaks of the results of brainwashing. As a child, she experienced the process by which Chairman Mao sold himself as a god. Jung Chang relates that her parents said, "'Do as Chairman Mao says.' And that reinforced the power of Mao's personality cult. Imagine a situation whereby you have no other input except Mao's words and only Mao as an object of worship. So it wasn't a belief that even went through my conscious thinking. It worked on people's subconscious so you grew up taking it for granted, you grew up knowing no alternatives. Sometimes I think it must have been as simple as a biologically conditioned reflex."

When I was nineteen, I worked as a stewardess for a charter airline based at London Gatwick. The first Tel-Aviv flight I operated was a real eye-opener—and that's putting it mildly. The orthodox Jews en route to the Wailing Wall, including the little boys, wore skullcaps over long strands of hair that hung in beautiful coifed ringlets. I had never seen such different-looking boys, and I couldn't help but stare. These passengers refused to make eye contact and stringently avoided any bodily contact with the female cabin crew just in case we were unclean (menstruating). When we handed them a meal, we were encouraged to put it directly on the lap tray, avoiding the possibility of our fingers touching theirs. From time to time, I contrived to hold the meal tray in such a way that my fingers might dust theirs, but the lightning reactions of the average orthodox Jew saw to it that I only *once* felt the skin of a "clean" fingertip. (If the man that I fouled is reading this, I would like to take this opportunity to say I'm sorry: I'm sorry.) The boys who accompanied their fathers would likely someday have boys themselves, and as we flew towards Ben-Gurion Airport, I wondered whether they would ever find themselves hopping on a plane, kicking off their Timberlands and relaxing with a gin and tonic. Would they ever leaf through a copy of *Sports Illustrated* while checking out what movies are scheduled? Would they ever ask one of the stewardesses for a phone number or chat to their neighbor about their upcoming ski vacation? Or did their conditioning forever mean their priorities would lay solely with expressing their faithfulness to Yahweh? For the most part, these devout men spent the entire flight pouring over their scriptures. As they read, they rhythmically rocked, just as my daughter does when she's stuck in the back of the car and needs to go pee-pee. As soon as the service trolleys were stowed, they would quickly head to the space next to the rear galley, in-between the left and right emergency doors. Small prayer mats would quickly be rolled out and the blissfully indifferent would drop to their knees, totally able to blank out the fact that they risked being trampled by the other passengers who were waiting for the loo. There they remained, in contemplation and prayer, until the plane's descent.

Like the Hasidic Jews, devout Muslims follow similar disciplined methods of worship. I joined British Airways in my early twenties and traveled further afield. I spent a great deal of time in Bahrain. The hotel in Manama was built next door to a mosque. Five times a day, a melodious sort of siren (a muezzin) would call Muslims to prayer. I'm not sure whether women were permitted into this mosque, but being a Western gal, I wasn't dressed suitably anyway. But after watching Arabic TV, much newsreel footage revealed the religious goings-on. Supplicants in this tradition seem to spend a huge amount of time standing, then kneeling, then putting their arses in the air while keeping their faces and hands on the ground. So it went, endlessly: standing, then kneeling, then putting their arses in the air while keeping their faces and hands on the ground; standing, then kneeling, then putting their arses in the air while keeping their faces and hands on the ground. I felt dizzy just watching, darling.

It's quite probable that large numbers of Muslims are physically fit but what about their minds? What happens to the mind of a devout Muslim child? Does the pressure of absolute obedience to the rules, coupled with the aspiration of memorizing the Koran mixed with endless hours of prayer ever overwhelm him? And how much of the Koran is one supposed to know by heart, anyway?

In *Islam Revealed*, Dr. Shorrosh writes, "A Muslim theology student (I think that's putting it nicely) must complete a course of instruction in grammar, rhetoric, logic, law, and dogmatics before beginning the study of *Ilm-il-usul* (science and principles), the aggregate of the Quran, Tradition, Ijma, and Qiyas. A good memory, not judgment or analytical thinking, is the great virtue of a Muslim theologian." Now, I am not saying that the average Muslim theology student is going to become a terrorist, but I do believe a life of acute imbalance is the experience of any child who winds up a terrorist.

Apart from one's conditioning, what else might entice one to become a terrorist? Perhaps the notion that one's suicide would esteem one's family might egg one on. If you are parents of a Muslim martyr, your life might have been unremarkable when your son was alive, but the new status that his death brings, is (how can I put it) rather well regarded.

Jumping ship with the knowledge that doing so means a quick exit from a world he loathes is the primary concern of the average martyr, but he also happens to believe that fair maidens in thongs will greet him at the pearly gates. Muslims refer to heaven as the "Gardens of Paradise." This reverie is mentioned in nearly every chapter (surah) of the Koran. With testosterone levels raging, the big hook is the never-ending supply of horny young gals along with the promise of getting permanently laid. (If my husband were promised the chance of getting laid three times a day for all eternity, he'd do anything too.)

If the fanatical Muslim youth understood the true premise of his existence, *that* understanding would end the bitter disappointment he might face upon realizing that the Heavenly Hilton doesn't have a maid, mini-bar, room service, or Netflix. And there will be no Kim Kardashian look-alikes feeding him grapes on satin sheets either. There won't be much of anything that holds promise because I doubt whether suicide offers one an escape. *Any* terrorist who thinks suicide will bring him either total freedom from pain or a blessed afterlife might immediately find himself back down here on the stinking planet that his warped slant on God *helped* create. He then might find himself looking around and thinking, *This cannot be the best God could do!*

The Big Three preach the smallness of this life and everyone in it. Earth is simply a transit stop. Entry into heaven, our cosmic reward, is the climax of all that we struggle and strive for, and this *great monotheistic belief* has caused humanity a lot of problems—none of which show any signs of alleviation. Indeed, the crux of Muslim spirituality seems to spotlight the "wonder" of the paradise that follows—to rather chilling degrees. Sam Harris, in his vital book *The End of Faith, Religion, Terror, and the Future of Reason* speaks of the political predicament that the Western world faces when dealing with a race of people who adhere to religious ideas "that belong on the same shelf with Batman, the philosopher's stone, and unicorns." Harris goes on to say, "It should be of particular concern to us that the beliefs of Muslims pose a special problem for nuclear deterrence. There is little possibility of our having a cold war with an Islamic regime armed with long-range nuclear weapons. A *cold* war requires that the parties be mutually deterred by the threat of death. Notions of martyrdom and jihad run roughshod over the logic that allowed the Unites States and the Soviet Union to pass half a century perched, more or less stably, on the brink of Armageddon. What will we do if an Islamic regime, which grows dewy-eyed at the mere mention of paradise, ever acquires long-range nuclear weaponry?"

I suppose the consolation of paradise is the cosmic comfort-blanket, clung to by those Muslims whose lives present to them an uphill battle of hardship, especially the women! Maybe the doctrine of an eternal reprieve from the challenges of Middle Eastern life does help one get through the day. But the bummer of all bummers it would surely be to arrive in heaven only to realize that a lifetime of piety and subservience to every male, were not on Allah's top ten list of must do's. To realize that Allah didn't care whether one wore a burqa, or a bikini, would no doubt have infuriated Fatima, deceased wife of Mustafa, daughter of Abdul. Did she stamp her feet before crying out to her daughters—*wishing* they could hear her? *"Acquiesce to your men, no longer, and close that damn book, it's not infallible."*

I would like to send a little message to Fatima, and all the other Muslim mothers of this world who give birth and hand over the raising of their sons to their blinkered husbands: *You know who you are. Review your religion. Unite, rise up and rein your fucking men in. There's an imbalance in your neck of the woods, and you need to take care of this shit because it is now affecting the rest of the world. Yin without yang, and vice versa, causes discord and not much else.*

CHAPTER FOURTEEN

God Has Favorites

God *prefers me, nah-nah-nah-nah-nah,* is the monotheistic mindset.

Islamic fundamentalism is on a crusade to convert the entire world to the only religion of which they believe God approves. Islam apparently holds a special place in our maker's heart, and as far as they're concerned, Allah believes the rest of us are worthy of little more than contempt. The Christians believe that God is going to pick all those who are saved. Those who sincerely believe that God is this second-rate jerk insist that He is going to say, "Kiss my arse" to all those who didn't. And the fact that the Jews refer to themselves as God's chosen people pretty much speaks for itself.

To believe *any* of the above is to believe that God folded His arms and scoffed at the Eskimos, scorned the American Indians and said, "fuck you" to the Hindu's! Did He turn His back on all Buddhists, the tribal Africans, and what about the billion or so Chinese? Did He wrinkle His nose up at the Aborigines and say "yuk" to the Maoris. Did He then proceed to stretch His doting arms towards the Jewish race, who, reveling in their specialness, believe that God ear-marked them for favor by asking that they lead the rest of us to moral eminence? Establishing themselves as being God's VIP's, the Jewish people believe that God pretty much said, *Revere the Jewish people or deal with my wrath.* Genesis 12:2-3 tells us of an exchange between God and the Jewish forefather, Abraham. "I will give you many descendants and they will become a great nation. I will bless you and make your name famous, so that you will be a blessing. I will bless those who bless you, but I will curse those who curse you." When the monotheistic God of the Jews pronounced His grandiose vision for Abraham, He basically makes the outrageous declaration that Judaism's "enemies" are inferior and potentially blighted. Hang on a minute. That's me God's talking about.

Charmed, I'm sure.

Perhaps some of my readers are once again apt to ask, "By what method has Sarah Tirri, in contrast to the Jewish, Christian, and Muslim religions she berates, come to know the mind, nature, and attributes of God?" Faith. *Faith* is the answer. I don't believe God has favorites because I have faith in a magnificent God who created a world of equality, choosing and favoring everybody. Despite the monotheistic slant on the *preferences* of our creator, I see God in a very different way. I know God is a God of magnificence, because every time I look at my sleeping children I am reminded of this. My children represent God's magnificence. He wouldn't have been able to create their perfection if He Himself were anything other than that. Fine wine, lump crab, and passionate sex with the man I adore is another reminder of God's splendor. When I arrange 200 thorn-free roses while listening to The Moody Blues' greatest hits, it is clear to me how misunderstood God's enormity is. I know there are no limits to what God created. That's why Kendall Jackson's reserve chardonnay tastes so good. My mother and father would never have been my parents if God had done anything with limitation, and when the sun sets in the Green Swamp, I am reminded that a beautiful order exists in this universe, because the God who created it wasn't the choosy little shit that the Big Three turned Him into.

The average mother walking around Jerusalem might hope to lead a happy life. She won't, of course, because someone she knows is going to die in a bloodbath and she will feel anything *but* happy. With a weary look, the BBC will film her sidestepping the latest bombing disaster, glaring at the men who dare to claim they represent a God who picked favorites. If he survives to manhood, her son will grow up to a life in which God has been packaged as having favorites, and those who think *they're it* will go to war over their belief. The monotheistic trinity—God help us!

The monotheistic worldview belongs to the people who think nothing of murdering their enemies even though the basic worldview of the people they are murdering is the same. They'll do it in front of women and children, and they won't care who gets maimed in the process. The in-fighting of the monotheistic factions is nothing new—the fanatical mindset: Jews verses Arabs, say, or the Catholics versus the Protestants, or the Sunnis versus the Shiites. Men of monotheistic persuasion are murdering in retaliation, vengeful, fearful men who breathe down each other's necks with hate and condemnation, blindly following the doctrines given to them at birth. Their God doesn't flinch because He too has murdered. Besides, a little bloodshed here and there will get us all used to Armageddon anyway. History is on course. God backs the victor, and the Jews believe it's them. So do the Christians and so do the Muslims.

Watch the evening news. Time after time, you will see journalists reporting mayhem from the Holy Lands. Here, God is simply a reflection of those who think small and behave small. We have three factions of the *same* monotheistic worldview manifesting the conditions that make this world unstable. Judaism, Christianity and Islam: The people who create instability in this world worship a monotheistic God.

CHAPTER FIFTEEN

Behold: A Godless World

The Big Three sold the ancients a phony premise of human smallness—which has been hauled to the present day. But many along the way balked at the teachings of religion and regarded the views of science as superior. And what we are now left with (in large numbers) is the worldview of mechanistic science—the atheist. The atheist: a man who sees a Newtonian world as one big fat godless machine. To my way of thinking, the views of the atheist and those of the monotheist are not unalike. Both share as the core of their beliefs, its essence, human smallness.

Actually, the atheist is not solely a creation of a mechanistic worldview. Many atheists have become just *that* because they cannot reconcile suffering with the bullshit they had been previously sold about God and creation. They cannot believe in a God who would put them through the torturous process of life while seemingly denying them the ability to be able to forgive. How many atheists out there possess deep wells of undiffused pain that prevent them from seeing a happier world full of magic and purpose? Along with Christianity's narrow view, the atheists' equally narrow view of reality is the great Western affliction.

Mechanistic science.

During the eighteenth century, which is known as the Age of Enlightenment, we decided to reject the church as the sole teacher of this curious world and handed it over to science. We'd had enough. Something had to change. We needed to know more. In science's application of reason, God was dismissed to the mystical realms of philosophy.

Religion birthed science because there was obviously something we were not getting. Traditional science was born and reported its findings without any regard for the spiritual. Traditional science decided it was its job to investigate reality without the premise of divinity interfering with reason. Science then became the universally recognized authority, and humanity became dependent upon its verdict to prove all aspects of our existence.

Monotheistic religion couldn't answer our questions, so we relied on people like Sir Isaac Newton to tempt us with a new view. Science, of the mechanistic kind, then proved ultimately that it too was only able to offer us more of the same. Monotheistic religion seeks smallness, and traditional science cannot, premised upon the dictates of the five senses that characterize its exploration of the world, escape smallness, so our belief in smallness shines.

God must be doing His nut! Has He ever looked down at all those who've assured the rest of us how *miserly* earthly reality is and spluttered?

"Hello monotheistic religion, the real God here. How dare you!"

"Hello everyone else. The Western world has for quite some time now been dealing with an organization that completely misrepresents Me and an organization that completely denies Me—therefore diminishing you. But it's now time to shake off any residual notions of human smallness imposed on you, firstly, by religion, and secondly, by an intellectual body that you assumed would save you from the mess made by the former.

Man cannot live on science alone; you tried for a while, with the Big Three smiling sweetly, cheerleading your efforts. For hundreds of years, traditional science knew no bounds, and you have evolved because of *science*, but now, ironically, have overtaken its boundaries."

"Hello traditional science. You have done a fantastic job. Thank you. I really mean that. But you really must concede that a little more expansion is now necessary. Your traditional ways have outlived their usefulness. Give it up… Oh, sorry. I see some of you have. Excellent."

The viewpoint of men who limit their thinking to tedious godlessness is something that evolution will weed out, as it *will* weed out the viewpoints of men who possess the "big God–little human" mentality. These views diminish God's creation to sorry-assed levels of pitifulness and are an attempt to counter evolution—ultimately and always an unsuccessful pursuit.

My husband doesn't like to consider more expanded spiritual concepts and has likened all spiritual thought to hogwash. A quintessential error that afflicts the thinking man is his belief that religion and spirituality are to be compared. Such a comparison does nothing but force a thinking man to live with tunneled vision. The inability to think freely happens next, and ignorance flourishes. (I love you, with all my heart, sweetie. I truly do. But when I need to vent, I do so on paper—that way you can't baffle me with your logic.)

My husband, who's a Vulcan, doesn't subscribe to the teachings of the Big Three or any other religion. He is what is popularly known as an atheist. I have heard the word atheist defined as "a man who believes himself an accident." Or perhaps he was the young boy, expectant and trusting, who found out when he was ten that Santa Claus was Mommy and forever refused to be hoodwinked.

My husband doesn't believe in Santa Claus, and he doesn't believe there's a God. He does, however, believe that we live only one life, which is the same doctrine taught by the Big Three. He poo-poo's any alternative to the Western premise, and he and his family members ridicule the Western church with scathing condemnation, refusing to say, "Okay, if this is all bullshit, let's find something that isn't." They just turn the other cheek atheist-style and hope the premise that they've assumed underlies existence will bring happiness and fulfillment. It won't, of course, because there's only one road to happiness. The journey might differ somewhat, but all men are equal in their common destiny. All men will come to understand that their thoughts are creating manifest reality.

The atheist mentality is a backlash brought on by the bogus teachings of monotheistic religion, but it's not enough to condemn something and then conclude that questions such as *what are we doing here? why are we doing it? and how does the doing happen?* are irrelevant.

Why are we here?

My angel, Aunty Joan, who I lived with as a teenager, was a devout Christian and her husband a devout atheist. Both had no idea *why*. Aunty Joan felt her life situations were unfathomable and uncontrollable. After she died, Aunty Joan left me her Good News Bible. In it I found a piece of tissue that marked the page she was reading. There was a pencil mark in the margin next to Psalm 22: *"My God, my God, why have you abandoned me?"* She felt God's presence strongly but couldn't comprehend why so much shit happened to her. She's not alone in this regard.

The Belizean mother who, just last week, lost her fifteen-year-old son in a drive-by shooting, has no idea why either. She asks herself this every day, and no answers come; she lives in the Christian/atheist culture that will not—cannot—provide her with an adequate answer. She's going to spend the rest of her life waking up on a damp pillow because she has no idea why.

Ruben has no idea why. Ruben lives in South Central Los Angeles. His father left the home when he was two, and to support Ruben and his five brothers, his mother works her fingers to the bone in a meat packaging factory. She has no idea why.

Nigel shoots his veins full of heroin because he has no idea why.

"Why do I feel like this?" Victoria screams. But it's too late. The fast train from London can't slow down in time. A few years ago, my brother, who drives trains for a living, plowed his 100-ton beast straight into Victoria, who had no idea *why*. The depth of her ignorance was represented by her mangled body. Not knowing *why* creates powerlessness. If you don't understand why you are here, how it happens, or why it happens, you are not going to be able to grow. In fact, you'll be busy just trying to hold it together. Some, like Victoria and Nigel, don't even manage that.

I recently experienced a four-hour stint in the emergency department of my local hospital. My daughter had broken her arm. I sat opposite a lady whose disposition was friendly and very immediate. She was one of those people we're inclined to brush off because we think they might reveal their embarrassing life story all too quickly. She did. Robin was her name. My daughter sat across the room watching cartoons and coloring, and I had plenty of time. I knew Robin was looking to off-load, so I asked her a question that opened the floodgates. She told me that the neighbors suspected her of abusing her nine-year-old son and had called the Department of Children and Families, which sent an inspector to her trailer. Her son was removed and put in a foster home for six months while she cleared her name. The events that have happened to her and her family during that time were so appalling that I wasn't sure she was actually speaking the truth. I suppose if I had spoken with her ex-husband he would have had a different story. But I *am* sure of one thing: If I had asked either of them what they were doing here, why they were doing it, and how the "doing" happens, neither of them would have had the faintest idea.

The day after this, I called my mother-in-law and told her that I had a question for her and would write down her first answer. "Why were you born?" I asked. Without delay, she replied, "I have absolutely no idea." The following week, I sat next to a man as we watched our children practice their strokes in their swimming class. I asked him the same thing, and after several seconds of careful thought, he replied, "I really couldn't tell you." I have, in fact, asked quite a few unsuspecting people this ultimate question: *Why were you born?* "God knows." "Couldn't tell you, love." "I dunno, really." "Well, there's a question." "You got me." "I haven't the foggiest idea." Some people would quickly launch into an answer, but in all cases, their response rapidly fizzled into an embarrassing recognition of the fact that they couldn't actually tell me. Nobody was able to tell me. Nobody. Am I the only person who thinks this is really weird?

Now, some of my readers might declare that the question remains how—if at all—does this failure to answer such an important question reflect on "monotheistic religion"? Here's how: The premise of monotheism, a worldview belonging to much of the Western world, does not reveal the truth behind what we are doing here, how the doing happens, or why it happens.

Look around. This is not the best God could do. Atheism does not reveal the truth either, for all is random in the atheist's little world. So, when nosy women like me ask questions like "Why were you born?" there are not many people who can answer.

As author C. S. Lewis put it, "If we have no notion of why things happen, then, of course, we know of no reason why it should not be otherwise, and therefore we have no certainty that it might not some day be otherwise."

What our parents held as their worldview pretty much determined ours because what we believe will be bred into the future generation. And as Robert Green Ingersoll said, "If we don't question anything custom will meet us at the cradle and leave us at the tomb."

There are many parents who don't have any particular spiritual opinions. I know my parents didn't. I had to wing it. I was offered the Western à la carte menu of belief systems and took my pick (holding on only until each one no longer served me):

The Adam and Eve rib story.

The random evolutionary/mechanistic science story.

The "No, there's not, and who gives a fuck anyway?" atheist story.

The "There might be a story, but I'm so focused on the external that I'm not prepared to look right now," me, me, me story.

The agnostics have a story too. It says that God is unknowable. (And that's the most hopeless of all the stories.)

Most children will follow the religious persuasion of their parents, which is fine, except when our parents fail to pass on anything of real value to us. This unfortunate hand-me-down means we have to learn the hard way. My parents unwittingly bestowed ignorance on me, and I didn't ask this big question of them. Or maybe I did. I can't remember. Maybe, at the tender age of five, I tugged on my mother's blouse and said, "Why was I born?" And as she applied her lipstick, maybe she responded by saying, "God knows! Now blow your nose, Sarah, and listen out for the doorbell—the babysitter is on her way."

Maybe I asked my father, "Why am I here, Dad?"

"You are here to enjoy yourself, Sarah. Now, come on, I've found this great little pub just outside Weighbridge, and it has an outside play area for kids—you'll love it."

Maybe, while visiting my grandparents, I walked into the kitchen to ask my grandmother the same thing, but the tired look in her eyes as she mashed the potatoes stopped me.

"Except ye be converted, and become as little children, ye shall not enter into the kingdom of heaven," said Jesus. But what does Jesus really mean by this, and what is the kingdom of heaven?

Other than *no, mine,* and *ut-oh,* the word my children learned earliest and used the most was *why.* Here's a typical *why* mommy/child exchange that I experienced over and over again:

"Charlie, put your jacket on, darling."

"Why, Mom?"

"Because it's cold."

"Why is it cold?"

"Because the sun isn't shining and the wind is strong."

"Why?"

"Charlie, let's ask Daddy when he comes home; he's a pilot, and he knows more about weather that I do."

"Why does he know more about weather than you do? Is Daddy *cleverer* than you, Mom?"

"No, darling, he is not *cleverer.* It's just that people have different abilities."

"What does "bility" mean?"

"It means, Charlie, that I have the ability to get cross if you don't put on your coat. Now, come on or we'll be late for school."

"Why will we be late for school?"

"Because I said so, that's why."

For some reason, the "why inquiry," which belongs to our childlike nature, wears off. Perhaps being late for school takes priority over wisdom, who knows? *Unless ye become as little children, ye shall not enter into the kingdom of heaven.* Is asking *why* the childlike state of perpetual questioning that Jesus is referring to? And is creating the kingdom of heaven the purpose of our earthly evolution? What is it that God has in store? Maybe once we realize that we are divine beings who create our own reality, we can put this knowledge to good use. Is building the kingdom of heaven here actually what we have been doing since the big bang?

CHAPTER SIXTEEN

Big God – Little Human

God's nature was classified and then recorded in the Bible by our religious forefathers, who were succeeded by those *still* of monotheistic persuasion who decided to drag ancient concepts of this same God screaming into the modern world. The modern world continued to view God as omnipotent, and with the general characteristics of an average human male. Now, don't get me wrong. I love average human males, especially my husband and my boys, but it's rather freaky to think of God in the same vein. We are made in God's likeness. He doesn't have man's characteristics; we have *His*. Big bloody difference.

After attributing all sorts of human shortcomings to Him, we called our maker Yahweh, then God and later Allah and proceeded to war with each other for a very long time. And then, not too long ago, the Founding Fathers of white America hauled this same God across the Atlantic, but by setting up a federal government that had no *official* religion of which officeholders were required to be adherents, it could be said that religion didn't have much influence on this new nation. But the premise of our existence *remained the same*. Big God-little human.

Leslie Stevenson says in his book *Seven Theories of Human Nature:* "Even now, in some countries and in some areas, there is a socially established 'Christian' consensus… In the United States, there is an informal Christian ethos which affects the sayings (if not the actions) of politicians, despite the official separation of Church and State."

There might be an *official* separation of Church and State, but in God we trust—the *wrong* God. Now, trusting in this God might have been all right as evolution prepared us for greatness, but now we don't need to view God in the same way as our ancestors, who were unable to hurtle along a country lane in a 7,500-pound missile called a Cadillac Escalade while listening to their darling children argue over which movie should be played.

We are not subject to the same constraints as people like Ezekiel or Abraham—things are very different for us. We have zip-lock bags now. A government clerk in Tokyo can download the entire financial history of a bricklayer in Arkansas. We have created computers that interpret thoughts! I can order gourmet beef Wellington that can be packaged in dry ice and delivered to my front door. Abraham couldn't. He had to kill a goat for his supper. I can take an airplane out into the Everglades and fly faster than all the birds that are annoyed that their peace has been ruined by a noisy propeller. (And such a propeller would have enabled Abraham to reach the heights he had reserved for God.) Way back then, when ancient monotheistic man put together the official version of reality, science and information hadn't yet evolved. They didn't even know the earth was round and laptops and Big Macs were just marvelous creations belonging to a distant future.

We *are* the distant future. Divers delve deep into the oceans; some search for useful biochemicals, and others swim leisurely around shipwrecks in search of a piece of history. We built a tunnel *under* the ocean. We build state-of-the-art hospitals. We make fantastic flea and tick shampoo for our evolved pets, and I can now be 200 feet from my gates and open them by remote control. Furthermore, McDonald's can now tell me exactly how many fat grams are going to clog my colon. And if my colon does suffer this iniquity, it can be safely irrigated while I receive a cucumber and seaweed face pack. We have more than a notion of why things happen; we *know* how they happen and how to make them happen faster. Surely, if we can create a technologically-advanced world, we can just as easily create a spiritually advanced one. Isn't this just a question of breaking free from an obsolete worldview and understanding God in a way that the ancients hadn't managed?

Einstein once said *that a problem is not solvable at the level of consciousness that created it.* We are not the same. We are a changed species, an evolved species whose awareness of his environment has developed greatly—a different species evolving in exactly the same way as say, a fish: One day, a fish on the edge of an evolutionary breakthrough got washed up onto land. The fish found that it could get around (somewhat clumsily) by sliding. This sliding creature, at some point down the line, grew legs. Each of these creatures viewed the world differently. Drastically so. In terms of this type of transformation, we're no different really.

For the most part, it's the evolutionary process that reveals the truth behind God; it's the evolutionary process that allows us to physically participate in the ever-changing human experience. Consciousness is the inextinguishable, ever-developing part of man's nature, the ever-developing part of us that is the point behind our divinely-created evolution. If consciousness is developed and expanded through our awareness as based on the accumulation of experience, then I contend that the consciousness of modern man is more evolved than the consciousness of, say, someone like Jalam the Canaanite goat farmer, descendant of Abraham, son of Oholibamah, wife of Esau.

The exposure Jalam's life offered, and his awareness thereof, would have aided his developing consciousness, but his life expectancy was what, thirty years? And that's if he ate well, didn't get attacked by a rival clan, and the women of his tribe took good care of him. Those featured in the Bible were here for precisely the same reasons as you and I—to expand their consciousness—but Isaiah, Jeremiah, Ezekiel, Daniel, Hosea, Joel, Amos, Obadiah, Jonah, Micah, Nahum, Habakkuk, Zephaniah, Haggai, Zechariah, Malachi, Matthew, Mark, Luke, John, Timothy, Titus, James, Peter, and Jude lived a smaller experience. They hadn't created what modern man now has. So how could they have grasped the enormity of this earthly reality? I fail to see how it's even remotely possible for modern man to reach new heights by relying solely on the perceptions of ancient man. Ancient monotheistic man saw only facets of God—ancient facets. God's magnificence had only been on partial display.

Evolution, "A process of continuous change from a lower, simpler, or worse to a higher, more complex, or better state." —Webster's Dictionary

Modern man inherited a compilation of metaphysical theories formed by people whose experience of what God did was limited to the evolutionary stage at which they found themselves. If the same people suddenly found themselves immersed in our reality—my fucking God! If Abraham the wonderful Mesopotamian nomad, the patriarch of monotheism, and his equally wonderful bride, Sarah, had been brought forward in time and given a VIP tour of Versailles, two things would have happened: Abraham's mind would have fried, and Sarah's would have told her, "This is a fabulous place; I must be in one of God's many mansions." Neither could have imagined the whims of Louis the Sixteenth. Come to think of it, I don't think Louis the Sixteenth could have imagined the whims of Donald Trump.

We don't even have to go back so far. Fourteen hundred years ago, Mohammed, an orphaned boy born into medieval Arabia (enough to send anyone into a life of cave-dwelling and contemplation) is, according to the Muslims, the most recent of monotheism's great prophets. Mohammed, I believe, only partially realized God's magnificence, for two reasons: A) The premise of his existence was the small monotheistic one, and B) His consciousness was not comparable to that of modern man's because evolution means we grow as we learn. Now, don't get me wrong, I'm not saying that Mohammed didn't know anything. I'm sure he could have picked out a sharp sword, and I bet he knew a healthy-looking goat when he saw one, but if someone had gone back in time and plucked him out of the desert and stuck him in the middle of a revolving door or at the top of an escalator, he would never have been the same again. If someone had managed to take him to the London Underground to watch a passing train come whooshing through at rush hour, he would have had a nervous breakdown. If the same person had dragged him to Gatwick Airport for a bit of plane-spotting, he would have quickly and irrecoverably needed a straitjacket. Should we believe that Mohammed's monotheistic voice—or any other ancient's voice for that matter—can profit an advanced race that *they* would have fallen on their knees and worshipped?

We in the Western world must shake off all ancient notions of human smallness, sidestep the precepts of monotheism, and realize that we will continue to understand more about God the more we grow. Why? Here's why: Ancient man hadn't viewed the moon through a telescope, let alone walked on it. They'd floated on the sea but hadn't been to the bottom of it. Removing Jalam the Canaanite goat farmer from his mother's womb by Cesarean section without his mother bleeding to death was not possible. The world the ancients were born into had not yet produced Godiva white chocolate and raspberry ice cream. Tiger lily and freesia-scented candles? Who would have known? Scented toilet paper? What was that? Jo Malone bath oil? I don't think so! Human rights, equal opportunities, democratic governing, protective services, compulsory education, and the abolition of slavery all happened because our evolving consciousness told us that all this would improve the world for humankind. We were right, it did. And if any of you are still thinking, *On what basis am I to accept Sarah Tirri's assertion that only people with scented toilet paper can know God,* know this: We are growing continuously. Our consciousness is evolving. The consciousness of ancient monotheistic man might have been expanded enough to be of some sort of benefit to his contemporaries, but was it enough to be of help to modern man? I think not. I think the consciousness of my six year old daughter might help us more.

CHAPTER SEVENTEEN

Separate and Suffering

Some of you may still be inclined to ask, "On what basis am I to accept the words of Sarah Tirri—the one who knows the true nature and attributes of God? How does *she* differ from the monotheistic males of old?" Some of you may even be bristling with indignation because I, throughout this book, object to the monotheistic men who've claimed to speak in God's name, and you are unclear why you should accept as authoritative or persuasive *me* doing that. This is a monotheistic dilemma.

In truth, we should *all* speak in God's name, but if you are bold enough to do so in our day and age, make sure that you have got the right God. To speak of God in a way that diminishes His "plan for us" is a practice that is, and will remain, highly objectionable.

The monotheistic premise of human smallness speaks of our being lesser creations of a separate God who is shrouded in an unfathomable divine veil that we pitiful humans, with divine exception, are incapable of penetrating. But working out who and what God is depends on whether one believes the great mystery of life was designed to be just that—a mystery. God as a mysterious and somewhat unknowable being is a concept belonging to the monotheistic/agnostic premise of human smallness, which rebukes people like me. I can hear the skeptics now, saying, "How dare we humans get ideas above our station!" Or "Who does Sarah Tirri think she is?" A few hundred years ago, the whole "burn the witch" mentality would have ruined my day.

Now, some of my readers here might state that I address with mere flippancy a question for which any sincere reader will demand an answer. But let me finish. Monotheism, in supporting human separateness, is apt to claim that only a special few are selected by God and are to be considered authorities on spiritual matters. Divine inspiration under the monotheistic decrees of Judaism, Christianity, and Islam led us to believe that God's divinity shone vividly through some and not others. Throughout the ages, many a monotheist with a charismatic personality and an appealing way of expressing himself (and an army might have helped) became an authority. A few of these people would turn into great political leaders, great statesmen, great orators, and great entertainers. A few became religious leaders. It was the religious leaders who really got our attention, however, because everything they professed was unblushingly claimed to be divinely inspired. This impressed us—back then we were easily impressed. God's selective bestowment of disclosure and trust lay, we were told, with a special few. It didn't encompass the masses; we were separate creatures from the divine and too busy being wretched and mediocre. We revered these prophets, and their words screamed at us unwaveringly throughout the centuries. But here we are, centuries later, entering a new age. Divinity can inspire us all because we are *all* prophets. We can all know God because we are all emanations of Him.

Western humanity has been advancing towards its current experience restrained by the fact that anyone who came along to speak on the subject of human divinity was quickly silenced by the monotheistic monopoly. Thus the view of man as divine has traditionally been met with scorn and contempt. Philosopher Alan Watts sums up what we face when considering human divinity: "Yet in our culture this is the touchstone of insanity, the blackest of blasphemies, and the wildest of delusions. This we *believe* is the ultimate in megalomania—an inflation of the ego to complete absurdity."

Realizing the God within is in fact self-realization, and that can take a while—and if you live in the confines of the Western premise it can take *a lot longer* than a while. Divine expression is something that Western humanity has spent millennia subconsciously trying to master in a culture that simultaneously and vehemently encourages us not to. Along with religion, traditional science has helped mold our beliefs, not out of any particular desire to blind us all to our divinity, but to deftly sidestep it, sustained by the Newtonian belief that the world is just a big, fat machine. From the absorption or rejection of both worldviews, we found our niche, but it wasn't a very big one. We had no idea of our *true* magnificence and evolved accordingly.

To believe in the concept of human bigness is to dispel the monotheistic notion that God is a separate being dwelling in a cloud of distant bliss. And to my way of thinking, God dwelling in a cloud of (exempt) bliss might be all well and good *if* the world He created didn't have to deal with so much misery. In fact, the concept of a separate monotheistic creator would be worth entertaining *only* if all of His creations led lives of illumination and contentedness, which is clearly not the case. For us to embrace a creator at all, He would have to experience the same problems that we do. But if He did, He wouldn't be separate. The thought of God lording it up in paradise surrounded by heavenly delight makes me want to scream. Who the hell does He think He is?

"Hi monotheistic God, Sarah here. If for some freaky reason you're a separate God, you're gonna have to get your fucking arse down here and experience a day in the life of someone who doesn't "get it" before my contempt for you even vaguely wanes. Perhaps you would like to watch your child die of leukemia. Perhaps you would like to endure your teenage years in Auschwitz and then at the age of 79 watch your house burn to the ground knowing that your two beloved cats are trapped in the front bedroom. Perhaps you would like to watch a jet fly into a tall building knowing that your wife is working on the top floor. Perhaps you'd like to have your children stolen from you by your ex-husband and not see them again for thirteen years. Perhaps you would like to witness your entire family drown in a massive tidal wave. Get down here you coward!"

Glorifying a separate God who created a world of so much suffering has affected our subconscious perceptions of life, and by definition subconscious fear, if not recognized in our conscious mind, will remain unexamined. This bogs us down. We are a bogged-down humanity whose divinity is only on partial display. Separation has many synonyms, all of which are quite depressing. The feelings of division, estrangement, severance, alienation, disconnection, isolation, disjointing, and parting all harrow the human psyche. We don't thrive under these conditions. Separation doesn't allow for expansion. In nine out of ten cases, separation induces constriction. In fact, when one (subconsciously) feels *plonked* on a planet without the foggiest idea of why, constriction can become a prominent theme, for if we have no true notion of the premise of our existence, constriction is basically a survival mechanism. Now, I can hear some of you saying, "I don't feel this way. I don't live this life of constriction that you're talking about." Well, picture the following: One day you close your eyes, and when you wake up you are living in a world of which you have absolutely no recollection. But you learn to adjust and things become typical.

You still have no idea what you're doing there, why you need to be there, or why things happen the way they do. Subconsciously, you're living in a state of fear, but the fear gets buried because, hey, there are places to go and people to see. You'll occupy your time with experiencing all this world has to offer, but you'll remain ignorant of life's true potential because the *laws* that govern creation (manifestation) were never addressed and no one ever told you that *you* had the same powers as God. (This happened to most of us the moment we were born.)

You see, to believe in a spiritual separation not only implies disconnection from the divine—it also implies dissimilarity. To believe we are different from God diminishes our idea about who we believe ourselves to be. If we fail to understand that we possess the power to manifest external reality and that reality creation is what we are doing minute by minute, (albeit within the physical limits of space and time), we won't know *why* or *how* this earthly reality is happening. What we see all around us is unconscious creation, which is a watered-down, fearful experience that powerlessness always generates.

Not only has the monotheistic idea of a random reality generated powerlessness, it has wounded man's capacity for reverence as well. Many don't revere life as the piece of magic that it is because they simply see God as a voyeur who created a rather hostile little species who suffers (limitlessly in many cases). I have a friend who sees a separate God as nothing more than a cruel bastard, and if he were writing this, he certainly wouldn't be using a capital G. My friend suffered horribly as a little boy and has not found *any* inner peace. He has not found *any* meaning as to why he feels so damaged, and he still suffers. All the time. Now, he is a man who is prepared to recognize openly that he can't stand life. Others pretend they live by choice and that they like it. They attempt to stage-manage what they secretly consider to be an unsympathetic reality, and what returns to them is a mirror of their beliefs. My friend has not gleaned any comfort from the monotheistic message that *He is one of God's children and God has a plan for him.* My friend maintains that, if a separate God allows the suffering of even one child in the name of some unfathomable divine plan, then the ends don't justify the means. I agree with him.

Some might counter this assertion by pointing out that suffering strengthens us. They might suggest that I at least acknowledge the arguments of those Christians who attempt to reconcile the conflict between the goodness of God and the suffering of the world. "Christians certainly recognize the problem, Mrs. Tirri, but they don't see God's goodness and man's suffering necessarily as a contradiction. Maybe you should read C.S. Lewis' *The Problem of Pain* or Philip Yancey's *Where is God When It Hurts?*" I might also be encouraged to read the Bible, which I am told also recognizes the conflict in the Book of Job.

Fuck that shit.

Here's why: The only books I would ever consider reading that attempt to reconcile the monotheistic God with the Christian meaning of suffering would *have* to be written by those, who, unlike the above mentioned authors, had experienced betrayal, cruelty, degradation and brutality to the levels of depravity that most of us willingly dismiss from our minds. I am *not* talking about the type of suffering that most of us have endured; I, for example, tolerated a fair bit of childhood strife—strife that felt awful at the time but which ultimately empowered me. I am talking about the type of suffering from which there is little hope of return. I am talking about intense, hideous, extreme, hopeless pain (physical and mental) that goes on *all* around the world, *all* the time. The pain of someone, say, who lived in a remote Rwandan village and was handed an assault rifle at the age of nine and forced to kill his family by the rebel army that kidnapped him from the arms of his screaming mother. Or, say, the suffering of someone who had been sold into prostitution by her father and spent her teenage years performing in a wrestling ring in Bangkok, shooting darts from her vagina at balloons to please the excited onlookers. Or, the pain of *her* cousin who was trafficked into a life of servitude and shipped off to South America, having no choice but to succumb to long painful bouts of deviant sex for years before escaping, taking with her, Aids, a swollen belly, a looming childbirth and a future with nothing left to cling to—except a dead baby.

I'm not able to read, acknowledge, *let alone* be persuaded by the arguments of those Christians who attempt to defend "God's veiled plan of suffering" who haven't suffered deeply. I am not now, and will never be, swayed by the arguments of those who believe God sanctions suffering but He Himself is exempt from it. And I doubt whether I will ever be swayed by the arguments of those who say things like: "We are members of a fallen race Mrs. Tirri, and God doesn't promise an easy time, just a safe arrival." Or, "We should patiently wait for answers, recognize that life is primarily a great monotheistic mystery, and know that God in His mercy created the glory of heaven to eclipse any bittersweet memories of what came before." It might be very easy to reconcile humanity's pain with a benign smile—cordially lamenting, "Well, The God of Abraham has a plan, and we will all be stronger one day." But I don't think I could ever disrespect those who have truly suffered so flippantly.

Admittedly, those who *have* truly suffered in this world, might react to the monotheistic idea of suffering with varying degrees of receptivity. Some might view their monotheistic suffering as Satan's transient victory over God and hope that one day God does a better job of protecting His flock. Some, like maybe a person who has been raped by their dad at the age of eight, might deny God's existence altogether but continue to pray to Him just in case He can be petitioned to step in and stop the pain. Others might swallow hard, breathe heavily through their nose, and seek enough sensation to blot out the pain and hope to be taken into the blessed afterlife, an afterlife where they will no longer have to deal with the malice of their pedophilic father's throbbing erection and they will be rewarded for their endurance by a round of harp playing and the love of a God who Himself will never experience sodomy. Others might choose to accept the monotheistic version of reality, but only with contempt, telling God to go fuck Himself. They might then look around for someone to project their torment on—unable to break the cycle—like my friend mentioned above.

And then, there are people like me who dispel the monotheistic view of suffering and understand that reality is *not* created supernaturally, by the hand of a God who Himself (with glad tidings) chooses not to participate in the human drama. I also dispel the atheist view of suffering as random and meaningless because, if that's true, we are living in hell. And I dispel the archaic—the draconian—the antediluvian—the primeval—the ignorant—the you-have-got-to-be-fucking-joking view that our lives are forever being sabotaged by some evil (mythological) force known as Satan.

God is in control of everything He created. We are not a fallen race. We are a divine *evolving* race, and God participates in that evolution. We are here to learn that, as divine emanations of God, like drops belonging to a vast ocean, we are creating our own reality, as we go, in a world of duality. Suffering happens because we have unconsciously created the world of suffering in which we find ourselves—or we are experiencing the karmic reflection of previous unconscious creation. (*This* I address in my novel: *The Day She Cut God Loose*.)

CHAPTER EIGHTEEN

Godlike

The millions of Christians who believe we're descended from Adam's rib seem to have a hard time accepting the certain fact that we *can* trace our descent from monkeys. It's not a hypothesis anymore; we have proven it. So why *do* many Christians have such a hard time acknowledging what is irrefutable? Most of us hate to be wrong, and to relinquish a cherished idea hurts. We can't stand it. I know this because I sometimes suffer this self-imposed affliction to degrees that still make me gag. Many would rather chance ignorance than admit error. We defend our traditions because we have too much pride. Our inclination is to shy away from change because we have invested a lot of time safeguarding our ego's ignorance. It takes balls and a sense of humor to wake up one morning and accept the fact that one had it all wrong. To be wrong is galling, but it is also the reason that many look at the world and think, *Is this the best God could do?*

The Western world has some changes to make. We *have* to update our beliefs about the nature of this reality and what God did, because holding onto our current view of human smallness means the world will experience more of what it is experiencing now. By changing our beliefs free in the knowledge that we can renounce any worldview bound by habit, personal history, experience, or circumstance, we can abandon pride in favor of enlightenment and transcend the monotheistic idea of creation.

We must understand that our personal awakening is evolution at work and that evolution *is* the creation of a better world.

If we are all fragments of the omnipotent in creative genius (God), then we must all possess the same creative abilities. We might not be able to look into a chasm of darkness and say, "Let there be light," but we invented electricity and saw that it was good. Surely that counts for *something*.

God said, "Let there be a dome to divide the water and to keep it in two separate places." We build water towers and retention ponds. We're no dummies!

God said, "Let the water below the sky come together in one place so that the land will appear." Take a trip to the Bahamas and check out the plush resorts. There are loads of mini-islands protruding through beautifully landscaped swimming pools. Lovely little tiki huts appear in the middle of them. One can sip piña coladas while sitting on the anchored barstools enjoying the water as it rolls and lolls. We *know* how to separate water and create islands. We do it all the time.

God said, "Let the earth produce all kinds of plants." I've walked through the grocery section of many an American supermarket. I know what goes on. We've now produced the biggest gourds the world has ever seen.

God said, "Let there be all kinds of animal life." Darling, we can clone a sheep in a petri dish. If anyone thinks that genetic engineering is a crime, know this: We *will* create life. We're all fragments of God, and we're here to complete the journey of understanding our creative divinity. Of course we're going to create life.

We will be able to create life by stopping death. Stem-cell research will see to it that we find a cure for diabetes. Likewise,

Parkinson's disease, like polio, is not here permanently. We will create a way of preserving life. One hundred years from now the average male will reach the age of 202.

We have already found a way of blending the genes of a Nigerian Dwarf Goat with that of the Golden Silk Spider. A goat can now produce silk in its milk. This biodegradable silk protein, once refined, can be made into an inch-thick rope that will be strong enough to stop a fighter jet landing on an aircraft carrier. Ten years from now, perhaps cows can be milked for Chardonnay. Who knows? Creation is what we do; this is who we are.

Jesus was the human who came to be Western humanity's greatest role model. His position, status, and mission have always been distorted, but Jesus was indeed divine, just as he claimed, and so are we. Jesus came to show and teach us how to master life. He had powers to feed the 5,000 because He was what we shall *all* become. We might not be able to turn a couple of loaves into a banquet just yet, but with a little help from Betty Crocker, I can turn an unremarkable box of brown flour into double chocolate chip brownies in just forty minutes. We can't raise the dead, but we *did* raise the *Queen Mary*. That's a start, isn't it? We now manufacture Hydra Zen, Lancome's marvelous anti-wrinkle cream that our female ancestors would have clawed our eyes out for. We can do a lot more than we once could because we've been busy evolving. We're getting there, sweetie. Rome wasn't built in a bloody day.

We are *all* gods, and we *do* create. What we create gets bigger and bigger. We will evolve by creating and recreating until we get it. The longer we do it, the more we will grow. We are becoming more Godlike every day, and the further back in time we go, the more unbelievable our current reality would have been. To the ancients, the ability to talk to somebody 4,000 miles away would have been considered a Godlike achievement. The ability to send words to some distant land by pressing "enter" would have been considered Godlike. And zooming down to earth in a rocket with fire bellowing out its backend would definitely have caused a few jaws to drop. If 2,000 years ago, a rocket had landed at Cape Canaveral and seven astronauts, seven of us, had stepped out wearing puffy silver suits, our ancestors would have:

A) named us,
B) built an altar to symbolize us, and
C) sacrificed bleeding animals in our honor.

We would have been considered gods.

In the eyes of the ancient man, the genus that we have become would have elevated us to a worshipable status. We have powerful creative abilities that once would have been considered godlike, and this will not change in the future. We will become more godlike by creating bigger and better. Becoming godlike is our evolutionary destiny. We are a work in progress. We only have to look at how far we've come to know how far we're going.

CHAPTER NINETEEN

Alternative Thinking: A Head-On Collision with the Bogey Man

Some time ago, I met a good Christian lady. She can be a little hung-up at times, but then can't we all?! I really like her, and I am hoping we will build a friendship. She walked into my library and started looking at the vast assortment of metaphysical books that I have been collecting for many years. She was going through a bit of a meltdown, and I thought she should look for a book to sooth her soul. A title called *Living Presence* by Kabir Edmund Helminski caught her attention, and her hand wandered to it. She turned the book over and began reading the back cover blurb, which said, "Sufism is a centuries-old spiritual psychology…" She swiftly slid the book back on the shelf—like it had burnt her hands. "Oh no!" she whispered, and quickly walked across the room to smell the roses on my desk. *Strange*, I thought.

Most Christians will tell you that the Bible is the complete, all-encompassing, word of God, and that reading the works from any other spiritual tradition should be avoided. My housekeeper believes this with the same conviction as if she was pointing out that the sky is blue. For her, Christianity is the only religion that knows God, and that's it. Matter closed. She believes reading any book that is not of "Christian thinking" is potentially disastrous. Satan, after all, is always sitting on the sidelines waiting to commandeer our minds, and looking at any other spiritual philosophy is exactly what he wants. "It's his *way in* Sarah, don't be a fool."

My housekeeper is, in a motherly/protective way, simply warning me of the implications of looking elsewhere. She cares about me, which is greatly appreciated. But in wanting to extend this same type of spiritual nurturing, I must profess that the only implication of looking elsewhere is the promise of finding out what we are doing here and *why* we are doing it.

The proponents of Christianity, as broadcast by satellite across the entire globe, assert that examining any contradictory viewpoint regarding the nature of this existence means, chances are, that we are experiencing the effects of the "enemy," who can be fought off only by employing God's help as a countermeasure through ardent prayer.

If one day you find yourself pondering a metaphysical thought that is not in line with the monotheistic version of reality, perhaps considering something that is a little less narrow in its perspective—say something that Buddha, Lao Tzu, Ramana Maharshi or Paramahansa Yogananda taught—you need not head off to church worried about being *possessed.* Just consider that your discomfort, your fearful mindset, is the ingrained Christian response to your dissension. If one day you find yourself thinking, *You know what, I've looked at Christianity, and I'm now ready to look elsewhere,* don't think that God is going to inflict upon you His monotheistic punishment for dissension. For some, it is a legitimate fear though—the Bible speaks of God's snappy reaction to dissension, look at Lot's idiot wife, for example. She questioned God and quickly got turned into a pillar of salt. She would definitely have been better off keeping her mouth shut. Or did she simply look back when God had told her quite explicitly to look ahead? I can't quite remember what pissed God off so much. But you know what gets me? Why couldn't God have just smacked her around a little? Surely that's all it would have taken. A pillar of salt? Wow.

Anyway, as those wishing to explore more expanded concepts of reality begin their journey, I should warn them what they are up against. Any frame of reference that doesn't get Christianity's seal of approval gets the "Occult!" sticker slapped right on it. Christianity's label for a different way of perceiving the world reads, Danger: Occult. Enter at Your Own Peril! And the word *occult* might frighten you in the same way it once did me.

The true meaning of *occult* has been misunderstood by many, and Christianity's version of bogeymen and satanic rituals seems to be a popular definition of it. I have heard irate preachers broadcast dire warnings of what was perceived to be "occult literature." One dedicated an entire show to the dangers of our children reading Harry Potter because these wicked books could corrupt our children. But in the context of corruption, the same preacher failed to mention that certain representatives belonging to one of Christianity's largest factions have perpetrated true wickedness by sticking their penises into young boys' anuses. Yes, Reverend, malevolence can be found in every segment of society, not just the segment of occult theory whose teachings, incidentally, will threaten your livelihood.

Like the lady I mentioned previously, I too have experienced an irrational reaction from reading the written word. I was naïve and impressionable, what can I say. In ignorance and in line with Christianity's warnings, I'd always considered the occult to be the study of black magic spells and sacrifices. When I was about twenty-two, I absentmindedly pulled a book off my brother's shelf. It was written by Dennis Wheatley (1897-1977). He was a late-Victorian novelist, and his book contained four stories written between 1935 and 1970. *The Devil Rides Out, The Haunting of Toby Jugg, Gateway to Hell, and To the Devil—A Daughter.* It wasn't the title of the stories that pained me but what was written in the flyleaf. Wheatley warned, "I desire to state that I, personally, have never assisted at, or participated in, any ceremony connected with Magic—Black or White. Should any of my readers incline to a serious study of the subject, and thus come into contact with a man or woman of Power, I feel that it is only right to urge them, most strongly, to refrain from being drawn into the practice of the Secret Art in any way. My own observations have led me to an absolute conviction that to do so would bring them into dangers of a very real and concrete nature."

Wheatley's advice is actually a perfect example of the dire warnings that many religions, Christianity in particular, has used to steer us away from any alternative views of God. I closed the book, washed my hands, lit a cigarette, and for a long time afterwards avoided anything I suspected was "occult." Those seeking to know themselves have been encouraged not to—we've been steered away from any teaching that explores our bigness. I left Wheatley's book on the shelf, and to my great detriment, I avoided anything that might have helped me on this complicated journey we call life. I often look back on all that has happened to me, wondering whether things would have been any easier if I had looked at the "occult option." The question is certainly open to debate, but I do know beyond doubt that I would have liked the freakin' option. I chose not to even glance at something that I was told would be very harmful to me, until my mother died that is. At that point I was past caring.

I have now spent many years—and I consider them well spent—looking at the alternatives to our Western religion, and when I first heard that the exploration of a bigger God was occultist deviance, I nearly choked. I didn't realize it for quite a while, but as I searched for something that felt more like the truth, I was actually participating in a study of various occult theories as defined by the Church elders. You could have knocked me down with a feather. I have, thank God, gotten used to the idea. The occult is the study of our human potential, the study of our own powers of creation—powers that are part of our divinity. Occultism is a vast subject and the magnificence of love is the primary concern of the occultist who knows that humanity can heal itself if the *hidden* truth behind our existence is revealed. Occultism is a study of God without the dreadful limitations that our Western religions have imposed on Him.

Now, some might say this definition of *occult* does not correspond either to the dictionary definition or to the general understanding of the word, but know this: The word *occult* is derived from the Latin word *occultus*, which means "hidden." Our divinity is indeed *hidden*. We must redefine our understanding of the *occult*, and as we do this, we can rest assured that God and the magnitude of the reality that He created will be revealed.

Furthermore, what of the monotheistic assertion that occult study births malevolence? Well, the human condition implies that manipulation can be a choice for many throughout all areas of life, including the study of human bigness. I've met a few very cunning people whom I knew were capable of bringing their lower impulses into any given situation. There are manipulative power-hungry people who might be interested in broadening their horizons, and when we expand our horizons, what we manifest reflects our expanding psyche. The occult is not an exception. But know this: People who are in the processes of discovering their powers of creation with manipulation and harm as their agenda will not ultimately find what they're looking for, because love conquers all, and love is exactly the central focus of study when one explores the occult. The occult is a study of human magnitude. We are magnificent, and so is the God of love that created us.

CHAPTER TWENTY

You Either Believe in a God of Magnificence or You Don't

You were conceived, born, and developed mentally and physically, and even as this was taking place you had no memory of what came before all of it, if indeed *anything* did actually come before it. And all that development takes place *without* a set of instructions. You have to wing it—you have no choice. You have to navigate your way through an existence which is capable at any point of delivering every imaginable scourge: frustration, disappointment, loneliness, failure, defeat, rejection, betrayal, abandonment, self-doubt, self-loathing, addiction, injury, sickness, terminal illness, and these are the more manageable afflictions. You might also suffer the unimaginable. You could be assaulted or raped or tortured to death, or you could lose a child and have to deal with the worst of all conceivable torments. To top it all, the backdrop of the *inevitable* never goes away: you *will* have to watch one of your loved ones die and wonder whether you will ever see them again.

Like every human being roaming this planet, you were endowed with a powerful instinct to keep yourself alive. If this was not so, the planet's population would only be a few million because this self-preservation instinct means you have little choice but to attempt to function in this *always* challenging and formidable environment without taking the proverbial back door out of it all. That is, to use another metaphor, as you try to duck all the shit that's hitting the fan along the way, you might be *tempted* to jump off the nearest building, but because something internal demands that you resist the temptation, you likely won't.

At some point along the way, it is likely that you have been presented with a menu: there *is* a God, there *may* be a God, or there is *no* God. And after mulling these possibilities you construct some sort of belief system, a theoretical scaffolding of sorts that you map over your life so that you might more easily endure it as you try to make something positive happen.

Your belief system might consist of one of the following categories:

A) You are an atheist and so do not believe in the existence of God because you have been unable to reconcile suffering with the existence of a compassionate and caring creator. Even if your life is relatively appealing at given points, even harmonious, it is likely that you have at some point taken stock of life on Earth and surmised that no decent God could possibly have created such a monstrous world. Your belief system is that life is just a crapshoot and there is no rhyme or reason to any of it. You either hide out at home to shield yourself from the unpredictable unknown or you explore the world around you and do a lot of doing. If the latter, ultimately the data you gather has no greater meaning and neither do your experiences, and either way you just hope that luck is on your side because you have no idea why reality appears the way it does.

B) You might have deduced that God is a man-made delusion, and you might pity those who believe that some sort of transcendental reality affects conditions here on

Earth. If this is you, none of what I am about to write will interest you, let alone inspire you, because there is a limit to the possibilities you are open to considering. Therefore, just continue on with your exciting life or trudge through your meaningless one and enjoy a good lunch when you can.

C) If you are an atheist and fear has unconsciously set in, it could be that you possess the desire to take advantage of everyone and everything in order to feather your nest. You do this because your belief system has established for you a premise that offers no spiritual significance to life at all.

D) If you are an atheist and reasonably well adjusted, you might be a genuinely nice person, or you might be the type of person who goes through the motions of trying to be a genuinely nice person with a strict moral creed to assist you. But fear is never lurking too far away, driving your reactions to life in a way that offers little relief.

E) Alternatively, you might believe there is some kind of divine architect who has some plan up His sleeve for the creations He went to all the trouble of bringing into this world, but *that* mystery is impenetrable, and due to its complexities, is almost beside the point. You believe that God is capable of plopping you into some reality that you are incapable of fathoming, and you are (unconsciously?) very uncomfortable with this idea and find yourself (unconsciously?) functioning with a fear-tainted consciousness. You might now hedge your bets and opt to follow whatever so-called God-inspired rules and regulations appeal to you, but no doubt the ones offering a blessed afterlife as a reward for all the nonsense existence has thrown your way tempts you the most. You can then hope that the God you have *strained* to correctly worship spares you. If this is you, the possibility exists that you do not give a shit about the future of planet Earth, and perhaps you don't give a shit about a bunch of people you'll never know. I can understand your selfishness, in a way; life on planet Earth can be rough, especially when you believe it is a perversion of what God originally intended, and the notion that your God is willing to release you from it and fuck over everyone else is pretty seductive. (If you do arrive in Heaven as a result of believing Christianity's doctrine regarding life and death, you might hope that God expunges your memory in case one of your children fails to make it. If the Good Lord *doesn't* endow you with this precious mercy, you might not be that comfortable in Heaven.) Anyway, any religion that asserts God has a chosen people and the rest of us will be condemned for possessing a different belief system is not a religion, it is a cult.

F) You might believe in the validity of some transcendental reality but believe that life on Earth is somehow illusory, a meaningless extended bad dream, and when all is said and done, freaky and pointless. You either believe you will be reborn for another bout of illusion or, because of your hard won "spiritual detachment" and because you have perfected the art of using meditation to bypass the challenges the material world presents, you can get off the Wheel of Karma and be absorbed back into the Supreme Spirit from which you came. There is nothing to learn and nothing to be gained from your experience here and getting back into the blissful state you conceived existed prior to your karmic cycle is all you can think about. If this is you, then you must surely have asked yourself this question: *Why would God have set up the conditions of life on Earth just so it could be a place of relative insignificance?*

Building a belief system rather than inheriting one must surely be an advantage. I spent years as a "seeker," sifting through mountains of books depicting all sorts of spiritual ideas, until I called off my search. By then I had created a belief system that wasn't as fucked-up as some of the crazy ones I came across along the way. This is what I now believe: we are made in God's image and evolving into something "more," and we come and go on this planet to cycle through successive lifetimes because one little life is not sufficient to experience *all* we must know in order to get where we are going. Where are we going? Who the hell knows, but my belief system is maintained by a high degree of faith. I have faith in the idea that *what* we are evolving into is nothing short of AMAZING.

If eternity exists, then there is no such thing as a destination, just a journey. And if we *are* made in God's image and *are* continually evolving into something more, the possibility exists that we can upgrade the conditions on planet Earth as we upgrade ourselves. I have witnessed my own evolution in this single lifetime as Sarah, and I am thrilled at how far I have come compared to the ignorant and fearful little bitch I used to be.

Anyway, if we *are* evolving, this means the common scourges of mankind's existence can be eradicated. This is not a dull-minded hippy fantasy. If you believe in a God of Magnificence, and this God created a system called evolution, then creating a better world *has* to be possible for its conscious participants. A God of Magnificence would not disallow the biblical concept of Heaven on Earth.

Indeed, the possibility of Heaven one day existing on Earth is the hypothesis that underpins the belief system I have spent the last twenty years building. In order to build a belief system, you must keenly employ your intellect combined with the highest degree of faith you can muster. Having faith in the notion that what God did is so mind-blowingly fantastic it would make you squirm is the key to ensuring your personal reality, along with the collective reality you are immersed in, receives an immediate upgrade.

Recently, I listened to philosopher and neuroscientist Sam Harris interview clinical psychologist Professor Jordan B. Peterson on his podcast (then called *Waking up* and now called *Making Sense*). The interview, titled *What is True,* was interesting enough, but things really began to heat up when both participants began the process of conceptualizing the meaning of the word *truth*. That is, *what it means to say something is true or not.* The discussion started out routinely but turned into a fascinating but grueling debate that ended in a ceasefire because no further ground could be gained by either participant. Sam probably won the debate because he was able to wear Jordan out with endless examples of *absolute truth* that Jordan refused to grant and Sam refused to sidestep, but it was Jordan who was *really* onto something.

Absolute and relative truth exist. For example, every person has skin covering their body is absolutely true, and it is a relative truth that the vegetation growing on this planet is a shade of green because the vast majority of it is but not all. It is absolutely true to say that natural childbirth is agony for a woman, and it is a relative truth to say that unloading the dishwasher is a boring chore that can rip families apart. But forget about absolute and relative truth for just a moment in favor of a new category; Jordan felt that the most beneficial classification of truth was **Truth as Beauty** as it pertains to an existence that profits *all.* If something profits all, Jordan argued, we might want to assume it is the truth, or at the very least profiting all is a relative truth (it is obviously impossible, an ideal, to do this) as near to absolute truth as we can get. Whatever beauty *is* (and I am talking about beauty as a hypothetical spiritual principle in this case), we should incorporate it into a belief system and then proceed as if this *is* the truth. That is, none of us can factually confirm what is spiritually true, and so consciously creating a progressive belief system that benefits all is the best we can do. Also, seeing **Truth as Beauty** is the only way to be sure one's level of faith is impeccable and, therefore, the belief system built as a result is also impeccable.

After listening to Sam's podcast again, I re-celebrated the idea that defining **Truth as Beauty** is the essence of any progressive spiritual path, and then I popped the cork of a bottle of Moet. When beauty is the eventual outcome for every soul ever born, karma notwithstanding, which only makes the journey more complex and longer, we surely have to be on the right track. You either believe in a God of Magnificence or you don't.

We should be concerned about cults, about *any* belief system that shortchanges God's magnificence, but we should absolutely worry about how a belief system, when acted upon, limits, and therefore darkens the ultimate prospects for, mankind's evolutionary potential. The Muslim belief system, for example, suggests that God is either a complete incompetent or a complete bastard. If Allah was not *able* to defeat Satan, and as a result human beings must live in a defiled world ruled by some raging malevolent force, Allah *is* incompetent. If Allah *could* defeat Satan but is not *willing* to, and as a result human beings must live in a defiled world ruled by some raging malevolent force, Allah *is* a complete and total bastard. Either way it is logical that those adhering to this belief system feel that the only thing to do is to enforce strict moral codes of conduct so deviance (Satan) can at least be harnessed until Allah allows us to check out. Either way, within the confines of life on Earth infiltrated by Satan, a Caliphate is an attempt to control the hideous plight of human beings.

As misguided is the concept of God having "chosen ones," a tenet of all the Abrahamic religions, a spiritual belief system that does not promote inclusivity is utterly repugnant, psychologically depressing, and evolutionarily unviable. Conversely, when you build an inclusive belief system and take it to its logical extreme, it translates into Heaven on Earth, a biblical concept that sounds very promising. I am sure the Christian God is quite happy that, in this book of horrors, enlightened concepts were at least touched upon.

Also, logically speaking, when employing one's faith to the fullest extent and using it as a catalyst to build a belief system, it is easy to see that the concept of Heaven on Earth has to be part of God's plan. It is unlikely that God went to all the trouble of setting up this system just so it would end up being a place of relative insignificance.

With faith as the lynch pin, how do we build a belief system? Just extrapolate all the available data from *every* religious doctrine, idea, and spiritual philosophy that pertains to a God of Magnificence. In short, cherry-pick the good ideas and discard inferior ideas of God and His actions. And so, by sidestepping (for a while at least) the doctrines of the Big Three, knowing that the Age of Monotheism is over, our divinity can and will be made known. Then we can reinterpret and reintegrate the teachings of the Big Three, which are compatible with a new worldview of human magnitude. As we pull together a new worldview by synthesizing elements of religious, occult, metaphysical, and philosophical sentiment, we must not further short-change God. We must take the best from all our great thinkers, maintaining our faith, conviction, and belief that God has big plans for the entire human race and that the promise of evolution means that the Kingdom of Heaven can be built here on earth.

And remember, any religious doctrine that does not honor inclusivity should be discarded. Christianity's doctrine—*You get one life, you live it, and if you believe that Jesus died for your sins, you can score a place in Heaven when all is said and done*—does not honor inclusivity. People get left behind, sent to hell where demons line up and laugh for eternity. Tens of millions still believe that God damns a large percentage of his creations to a hell to burn for all of time. How could *this* God sleep at night? I can't sleep when one of my children has a fever.

In the belief system I have built, no soul will be judged and found wanting, let alone punished or in any way subjugated— even if they have used their free will so poorly it would make your eyes bulge. My novel, *The Day She Cut God Loose,* uncovers the implication of reincarnation and karma as it pertains to evolution. Is justice one of God's highest ideals? I think it is, and if not, it sure as hell should be.

It is my belief that we each have led many lives. Throughout history, you have likely been a soldier, a miner, a nun, a ballerina, a robber, a doctor, a prince, and a peasant—any number of identities you temporarily inhabited. But why do we come here? Why do we put ourselves through all this shit? Earth is a kind of school we visit from time to time, a temporary affair, and as far as I can tell, human beings are reincarnating in order to perfect their focus, and in doing so use their minds to call things in from the unseen (the Quantum field). In other words, to manifest reality as we are capable of envisioning it.

Believing that man is here *to call things in from the unseen as though they were* is an extremely powerful idea and happens to have biblical roots. Romans 4:17. (Good on St. Paul.) Conversely, this is also a powerful idea: what if our personal belief system is *causing* our personal reality to appear the way it does? What if belief is the raw material, the building block to "thought," and related thoughts interact to create a specific quantum (unseen) proto-reality struggling to become manifest reality? In short, what if *belief* is the cause and reality is the effect as it personally displays itself to each of us? What if we are creating reality with our thoughts without even knowing it? And what would it look like if we were conscious of this process?

I probe the theory of "reality creation" in my novel: *The Day She Cut God Loose*. I believe the ideas in it are sufficiently powerful that *your* personal reality will receive an immediate upgrade.

-The End-

Printed in the United States
By Bookmasters